Timelines of Terror

Timelines of Terror

*The Fractured Continuities
of Horror Film Sequels*

JOSH SPIEGEL

McFarland & Company, Inc., Publishers

Jefferson, North Carolina

ISBN (print) 978-1-4766-9165-7
ISBN (ebook) 978-1-4766-4923-8

Library of Congress and British Library
Cataloguing Data are Available

Library of Congress Control Number 2023006990

Front cover: The Ghostface character from the 2022 film *Scream*
(Paramount Pictures/Photofest)

Printed in the United States of America

McFarland & Company, Inc., Publishers
Box 611, Jefferson, North Carolina 28640
www.mcfarlandpub.com

Table of Contents

Acknowledgments

Christy—This book would not have been possible were it not for my wife, who set this entire venture into motion with the simple phrase "Have you ever thought about writing a book?" Her support through this entire process is something that I, in hindsight, should have put into our wedding vows.

Stella—She's my demon.

Brad—When this all seemed like a pipe dream, it took the encouragement of a friend I've never actually met: the ex-husband of the best friend of my ex-wife. Thanks for steering me in the right direction and boosting my confidence to actually carry this to its completion.

The Patrons—You are the one thing I never expected. A community of fans, of people, and of friends. You guys make me feel like I can do anything and that when I do, there'll be someone there to check it out.

My mom—You got me into horror in the first place by bringing me home terrible selections from the video store. There's no better remedy for a sick and ailing kid than kicking back and watching *Slugs*.

Nancy—Because I know you would have ordered copies to give to everyone you knew, and because we miss you.

Introduction

One of the most common complaints about the landscape of cinema in our current times is that everything is a sequel, a reboot, or part of some massive, interlocking universe. Trilogies and beyond are planned out from the start, with a huge selling point of most properties being how they tie into other preexisting properties.

But things weren't always this way. Oh, sure, everyone has always thought about sequels and ways to continue on their storylines, but it wasn't always so meticulously charted, with what I'm imagining are huge walls with thumbtacks and string leading to all the other story points that springboard from this central concept. And Post-Its. So many Post-Its.

You can usually tell this because of just how poorly those films would link together. You start watching a second part to a movie, and things are changed, continuity is revised, characters are forgotten, and whole plot points are simply dropped or forgotten. At times, it would appear as if the writers of the sequels didn't even bother to watch the preceding entry. At others, it appeared as if they were actively attempting to sabotage them.

These little quirks and improprieties of the form are something that has always fascinated me. I've always enjoyed how writers would have to try to pick up where the previous film left off and weave a new story. I've been trying to piece together the logic between franchise installments for the past several years on my YouTube channel, *Movie Timelines*.

The whole purpose of the channel is to take movie franchises from all genres and break them all down, from film to film, one entry into the next, and try to determine what kind of logic and continuity can be factored into it to bridge the gaps. Oftentimes, well ... there isn't any, but someone has to try to make it so there is, right? Some sort of crazy person with too much free time to spare, and a few extra brain cells that they don't mind killing off.

When the channel began, the purpose of the very first video was to try to make sense of the timeline of the *Friday the 13th* franchise, an infamously fractured framework of a story, and see if there were any way to place exactly when the individual entries occurred. Watching the series casually, and seeing them as they came out, there's really nothing unusual. But watching the entire collection of the films within a short period of time, you start to notice the cracks in the delicate fabric of the story that they're telling. Focusing on the time frames that they give you within the story, you start to realize that the films are taking place at least a decade in advance of the times that they were released, and that films that premiered in the '80s would have to have been set in the early 2000s.

In continuing the series, and watching additional franchises and trying to utilize their own internal logics, you start to realize that the whole process is similar to an elaborate game of Exquisite Corpse.

There's no way to say the words "exquisite corpse" without your mind instantly conjuring up visions of horror, even if its origins were far more wholesome. The phrase is actually the name of a party game, created in the early part of the 1900s by a group of Dadaists as a fun diversion. The game consisted of each player drawing a piece of a larger artwork, then handing it off to someone else. That person would then add to the drawing, however they saw fit, and then also hand it off, as each new player would bring their own twisted vision to the overall piece. The concept isn't too far off from the game of telephone, with each player passing on information, with the message getting more and more garbled with each turn.

The game has since been turned into an artist's exercise, a way to hone your skills while interacting with fellow collaborators, and has been used in everything from poetry to paintings to song lyrics. Notable authors who used the style were William S. Burroughs and Brion Gysin, who both modified the game to something called the cut-up technique, in which they literally cut up writings and pieced them back together to form random word patterns. Music fans will recognize the title from a Bauhaus song, which was apparently written using the technique, or as the title of a track from the musical *Hedwig and the Angry Inch*, although that particular instance doesn't seem to actually employ the stylings, just appropriate the name.

But when it comes to films, Exquisite Corpse doesn't seem to be frequently employed. There were a few projects of various genres that actually used the technique, but most of the examples with the words in their titles aren't actually making use of the style, just using the title. Not coincidentally, most of these are horror titles, because of course they are.

Ultimately, though, films in general actually do make use of the Exquisite Corpse technique, in a way. But it's not always so obvious if you're just watching a singular film. You see, because of the sequel machine or constant franchising of every single property in Hollywood, finding a film with a single entry is next to impossible. Everything is a piece of a puzzle, an entry in a long-running franchise, or a part of a greater cinematic universe. A movie that's a stand-alone piece of work with no sort of follow-up is becoming more and more of a rarity.

But here's the catch. Most of these franchises and long-form storylines weren't actually intended to be that way. Most of them actually were intended to be a single entry. Every filmmaker thinks about a sequel, but the logistics and marketplace don't always make it a possibility. But with success comes more entries, and with the low budgets that most horror films work with, it doesn't take much to turn a profit.

Let's face it. Horror fans may be the only fandom that doesn't care about the things that drive most genres. No one really pays much mind to who the lead actors of the films are. Some of the most successful fright flicks have had a cast of unknowns on the roster. No one knew who the actors in *Blair Witch* were before the film was released. Hell, with the possible exception of John Saxon, the cast of *A Nightmare on Elm Street* were relatively unheard of. When someone asks, "Do you want to go check out the new *Saw* movie?" in general, the first reply is not going to be "Well, who's in it?" The casts matter so little that even the actors playing the killers rotate from movie to movie. Consider the fact that there are currently 12 films to feature Jason Voorhees, in which only one actor played the role more than once (Kane Hodder, in four films). Ten people in total have inhabited the character, with the majority of horror fans probably only able to name two or three of those actors.

Honestly, horror fans don't even care how well the film is made, since some of the more notable and profitable examples of the genre were financed on a shoestring budget by a group of friends in a single location. Certain fans, myself included, actually enjoy this level of horror films more than the polished, big-budget studio pictures, and again, horror films seem to be the only genre in which this is the case.

Comedy films are dependent on the talent involved. People go to those films based on who the star is, and how funny they are. Romantic comedies and dramas are entirely dependent on being star vehicles, with the success of the films focused on how big of a name is featured on the poster.

But not horror. And because of this, horror movies tend to make a profit. And because of *this*, they tend to get sequels. Lots and lots of sequels.

The trouble with this is that most horror movies tend to end with the main antagonist being killed off. Good triumphing over evil and all that. It's not always the case, as horror probably has the greatest percentage of entries in which the villain wins in the end, but more often than not, writers for the follow-ups are handed some pretty wild scenarios that they then have to figure out how to rectify.

Hence the Exquisite Corpse.

To me, film franchises have always felt like examples of this technique, horror in particular, because of everything that I've said above. Each entry of a killer franchise tries to outdo the last, killing off the main baddie in a bigger, more grandiose way. It's almost like they're purposefully daring the next writer to come on board and come up with some possible method of bringing them back. There's even the occasional "final entry" in which the producers decide to kill off the franchise for good, even if they never actually mean it, and therefore tend to showcase a much more definite ending to their storyline, killing off the main antagonist in the most spectacular fashion they can think of. Almost like they're crossing their arms and saying, "There. Try to bring them back after that."

But of course they can. And they do. It doesn't always make sense. But that's the joy of the Exquisite Corpse.

Part of the fun of watching it all is trying to put together the pieces, which is what I have taken it upon myself to do. Over the course of the five years, I've watched films of all genres, including sci-fi films, comedies, and of course superhero sagas, and they've all shown varying degrees of distorted continuity, but none seem to draw the interest of the fan base as horror.

Maybe it's because comedy films are inherently silly, and because of that, no serious continuity is assumed, and when things don't make sense, it just feels like another part of the joke. Maybe it's because superhero films are prone to reboots and often completely reset origin stories, so fans are used to differences from film to film.

And, well, let's face it, most comedy sequels don't have to spend any time trying to undo the spectacular demise of their main character from the previous entry. Same thing with superhero movies, really.

But horror fans are rabid about the lore and backstory of their characters and the weaknesses of and ways to kill their favorite genre villains, and I count myself within their numbers, so I've always tended to show more interest in bridging the gaps between those films.

This book will be an elaborated discussion of what has been started on my channel, taking several of horror's biggest and most fractured franchises and telling the story of what links them together, trying to build the overall timeline. What did each new writer have to work with? What were the specific challenges handed to them? What insane scenarios did the previous film end with that they would have to miraculously weave their way out of? And beyond that, what changes did they make to the overall series, marking their own contributions to the storyline?

The most common thing said when discussing the continuity of films in a given franchise is usually that they're only movies and there was never meant to be any sort of sense linking them, since the writers were making it up as they went. I hear that a lot. Some people kind of dismiss the entire process, as if there's no merit to trying to figure this thing out, and that I'm wasting my time. Well, they may be right. Damn. They're right, aren't they? I just realized that they're totally right, and this is pretty much just a waste of my time.

Oh well. Too late now. Besides, it's fun.

All art is open to interpretation, really. Classic paintings have been dissected over and over again, with any number of meanings being ascribed to them. Each of these reads into what the artist intended, regardless of whether or not it was the actual message. A viewer can derive a great epiphany from a piece of art, and it may be personally affecting, even if it's a viewpoint that was never originally thought out. We allow this type of introspection and assumed intention with other aspects of art, but apparently stop short when it comes to film.

Sure, when someone tries to figure out the exact contextual meanings of a David Lynch film, nothing is really said. It's a given that someone is going to try to read into that, even if the readings weren't actually what Lynch was going for in the first place. That meaning becomes the intended one, retroactively. It shouldn't really matter what the genre is, or whether the subject is "highbrow" or "lowbrow"—or, in some of these cases, "unibrow."

Ultimately, it doesn't really matter if any of this continuity was baked in from the beginning. It matters how we, as viewers, view it through our own personal perspectives.

And this is mine. Uh … enjoy it?

CHAPTER 1

Friday the 13th

The *Friday the 13th* franchise began back in 1980 with the original film, directed by Sean S. Cunningham. The intention was to capitalize on the success of *Halloween* by creating a new slasher film, changing their setting to a summer camp. It follows the formula of Carpenter's film by starting with a flashback, then jumping ahead to what was then current times. Even though it's often referred to as a *Halloween* knockoff, there's not a ton of similarities between the two. *Friday* has some POV shots and the overall formula of the structure, but it's a unique setting, a vastly different type of killer, and 100 percent less Shatner mask. Regardless of that, it's hard to deny that Cunningham has outright stated that his intention was to emulate the earlier film.

The timeline begins right off the bat, as the film gives us a date on the screen, letting us know that we're set in 1958 at Camp Crystal Lake. This opening scene shows us a pair of murders before the opening title screens and then flashes ahead to what it says is June 13, also noting that it's the present day. If we're going to take the film at face value—because at this point, why not? It's not like the film has lied to us so far—let's trust it and figure that they were suggesting that it's set in 1980 and we've skipped ahead by 22 years. This is a fairly safe assumption to make, considering that June 13 was actually on a Friday in 1980, although, oddly, the film was released a month earlier on May 9, 1980, which seems like a pretty unforgivable offense. I'm guessing that's why they went with "present day" instead of saying "1980," because maybe they thought that audiences sitting in the theater on opening weekend would be confused that they were watching a film in a time period that hadn't happened yet.

We get some additional fleshing out of the timeline from a local trucker who tells a bit more of the backstory. It seems that one year prior to our opening scene in 1957, there was a young boy who drowned in the lake. The murders that we witnessed then took place in '58. He goes on to say that there were a series of fires at the camp in '62.

The film is famous for creating the formula for the series: a bunch of teenagers alone near the lake at night, being picked off one by one by an unseen assailant, which is coincidentally the same formula for ... well, every slasher film from this time period. One of the biggest claims to fame of this particular entry, besides kicking off the long-running franchise, is the presence of then-unknown Kevin Bacon and his blue Speedo. At the time, he had only appeared in a small handful of films, and it would still be a few more years until his star really began to rise.

The film takes place over the course of a day or two, with everything happening on the one single weekend. In terms of series continuity, it's actually a bit of an anomaly among the rest of the films, considering that Jason is not the primary antagonist, a bit of trivia that would eventually cost Drew Barrymore's Casey Becker her life in *Scream*. Ultimately, the film can be seen as a prelude to the proper story of the rest of the franchise, setting up the evolution of Jason as a killer, since the villain here is actually Pamela Voorhees, his mother. It's revealed that she is not only behind the killings in the present day, but obviously those in 1958 as well. At the film's finale, she's killed by Alice, this entry's Final Girl, as she's beheaded via machete. The film does close with a setup for further entries, albeit a confusing one, as we seen a young Jason pop up out of the lake to attack our heroine. The epilogue insinuates that it's just a dream, though. That seems likely, since we know that Jason drowned in 1957 and was apparently 11 years old at the time, so he'd be in his mid-thirties by this point instead of the younger man that we see. As a

Pamela Voorhees (Betsy Palmer), pre-decapitation (*Friday the 13th*, Paramount, 1980).

point of record, if Jason was indeed born in 1946, that would make him 34 years old, assuming the film is indeed set in 1980.

Some elements would go on to become important parts of the overall franchise, and the most relevant of these is the setting. The action takes place at Camp Crystal Lake, which is portrayed as a small camp sitting alongside a mid-sized lake. It was filmed at an actual camp in New Jersey, although the location is never outright stated within the film itself. But a good number of the elements that would soon become cornerstones of the entire series are all put into place here. Not only do we get the setting, but the overall mood of the unseen camp killer is born, a plot device that will remain in place even after the mystery aspect is discarded. We also establish the theme of teenagers being punished for sexual activity, although it's more of a central focus here, since Pamela is specifically killing the counselors because they were too busy enjoying each other's company to keep their eyes on her son. This film also sets up the minor hints of supernatural influences at the lake, which is definitely not strongly emphasized at this point but is still a small factor, particularly in the ending.

Of course, the overwhelming majority of critics tore the movie apart, criticizing its gratuitous violence and paper-thin plot. It drew a particularly high amount of scorn from Siskel and Ebert, who went so far as to print actress Betsy Palmer's address for viewers to write and complain about her appearance in the film. But these negative write-ups didn't dissuade audiences, as *Friday the 13th* was a surprise hit, pulling in close to $40 million in the U.S. and an additional $20 million from international release.[1] It's of minor importance that it got an international rollout, considering the film was an independent production that was not an established property.

The next entry arrived one year later, with 1981's *Friday the 13th Part 2*, because back then sequel titles were just the original film plus the number 2 on the end, instead of the retitling and subtitling that would later take over the genre. Sean S. Cunningham declined to return and the directing reins were taken up by Steve Miner for his first feature film.

The film opens with Alice, the survivor of the original film, still recovering from the trauma that she had endured. While on the phone with her mother, she seems to indicate that it's just a short while since the events of the last film, so this opening sequence takes place a little later in 1980. Before long, she's attacked by another killer, and we see Pamela's severed head in the fridge. It's still intact, not drastically rotted, which would seem to reinforce that it's soon after the first film. How Jason is able to find Alice is never really stated, nor how he was able to get there; I'm assuming that he's not really much for driving, and taking public transportation would likely be out. It should be noted that the original concept was to have Alice return to face down Jason, but actress Adrienne King only returned in this diminished role instead. Depending on which story you believe, this is due either to King's distaste for the series after an encounter with an obsessive fan, or to her being too demanding when it came to salary.

Next, we meet up with a new group of kids at a new camp. It's established that there's another camp called Camp Packinack and it's also on Crystal Lake, very nearby to the site of the killings. This isn't drastically against the previous film's continuity, but is slightly at odds with it, considering that no one ever seems to mention another camp just down the road, although it's not completely out of the question. The camp's leader, Paul, establishes several elements of our timeline while sitting around the campfire. He tells us that the opening scene of the film, Alice's death, took place two months after the first movie's events, which would place it around August or so of 1980. He also says that the Pamela Voorhees murders took place five years ago, giving us a pretty solid time jump between the two films, and presumably setting us in 1985. Since they're preparing for the camping season, it's assumed that it's around the same time frame as the first one, possibly sometime between May and June. Paul also upends our continuity a bit by introducing the idea that Jason didn't actually die back in 1957 and has been alive this whole time after all, and had seen his mother die by the lake. It's certainly a confusing plot point, since it would be assumed that Pamela would have no need for revenge if her son didn't die, but the movie doesn't dwell on that conceit at all.

And it didn't have to, since hundreds of online film theorists have filled in all those blanks for the filmmakers, myself included. There are basically two very different schools of thought as to what happened. The first is that Jason didn't die at all, and has been surviving in the woods by himself all alone. It's theorized that his relationship with his mother wasn't as rosy as everything would seem, and he chose to stay out in the woods, away from her influence. He still watched from afar, though, and seeing his mother decapitated drives him completely off the deep end into his murderous rage. Some even state that it's possible that some of the kills in the first film can be attributed to Jason and not his mother, although that clearly was not the intention of the filmmakers at the time. The other theory is that Pamela was dabbling in black magic, as evidenced by some of the oddly supernatural occurrences around the lake. Much later in the series, this is further backed up the presence of the Necronomicon, the book from the *Evil Dead* series, in the Voorhees family home. It's noted that Pamela may have been dabbling with dark forces to bring her son back, and that the killing of the counselors was more of a ritual, or blood sacrifice, required to bring him back. Her own death ended up being the final requirement, resulting in Jason's rebirth from the lake in the end.

Another element of continuity between the first and second films is the inclusion of Crazy Ralph, a minor but memorable character, again played by actor Walt Gorney. Even though five years have passed, he doesn't seem to have aged at all and is wearing the exact same outfit, because once he found a look, he stuck with it. After all, hats and leather vests never go out of style.

The biggest claim to fame here is that this is the film to finally introduce Jason to the series. If you're not familiar with the franchise and only know Jason from his pop-cultural persona, it may be off-putting to see him in this film, since he's not quite the mountainous man we see later. He's also missing his trademark hockey mask—that's not introduced until the third film—and is wearing a sack on his head, reminiscent of the villain from an earlier film, 1976's *Town That Dreaded Sundown.* Another thing that might stand out to those familiar with his later appearances is the fact that he's fast, and frequently runs after his victims. His strength level also appears to be lower than expected, matching that of an average man. Paul is able to hold his own against him in one-on-one combat, as opposed to the later Jason who can punch a human head off. His wardrobe is also markedly different. As well as

Jason Voorhees (as portrayed by Warrington Gillette) sporting the hillbilly look (with Amy Steel as Ginny) (*Friday the 13th Part II,* Paramount, 1981).

the previously mentioned sack, he's sporting a set of denim overalls over a dark blue plaid shirt.

Again, the events of this entry take place over the course of two days. Day one introduces our characters, gives us our campfire scene, and sees the death of Ralph. The remainder of the film plays out over the next day, ending that evening, with the epilogue taking place the following morning.

The finale of the film gives us some other continuity elements that play out in future films, as we get a brief glimpse of Jason without the mask on. It's a distorted shape, similar to the form we saw from his childhood, with long patches of hair hanging down. This version of the character can be discounted, however, since it's presumed to once again be a dream. Our Final Girl, Ginny, seems to have hallucinated this appearance and attack, similar to Annie in the first film. The manner of killing Jason here is pretty understated, with a simple machete to the neck area taking him out, a wound that seems serious, but clearly not fatal. I mean, not villain-of-a-slasher-franchise fatal.

Once again, the overall critical reaction was unfavorable, with most reviews focusing on the repetitiveness of the plot. This didn't stop the film from making a ton of money, even though it didn't quite make the impact that the first one did, cashing in to the tune of around $22 million.[2] This number was less than half of the original's take, but still amounted to a huge profit, considering that it cost a mere million and a half to make.

A third entry took no time at all, and one year later, in 1982, we got *Friday the 13th Part III*, in 3D. Miner returned to the director's chair, and in terms of continuity maintained quite a few links to the previous film while setting up new contributions to the series lore. It picks up immediately after the last one left off, giving us a view of Jason crawling away from his machete wound, basically proving that the ending of the last film was a dream. You see, in that little epilogue, when Jason burst through the window, the weapon was still firmly embedded in his shoulder. Here, right after Ginny and Paul leave, we see that he has removed it and crawls away, machete in hand. It's kind of hard to think that Jason would put the blade back into his shoulder before jumping through the window to attack Ginny, so that confirms it as a nightmare. I mean, we know that Jason is a bit of a glutton for punishment, but it's usually reserved for others dealing out that pain to him, instead of being self-inflicted. Early on in the film, there's a news report showing footage of Ginny being taken away to the hospital and they state that it's happening right now, so we're set on the very same as day as the final shot of the previous film. It's one day after, presumably still in 1985. Jason changes outfits, ditching the overalls look, but this film does actually go out of its way to explain the wardrobe change. Our killer is seen lurking outside of a home, amid the laundry lines. He's visible for a moment, still wearing his togs from the prior film, sans mask. A moment later, he's gone, as is a set of clothes that were draped over the lines. This is a pretty notable attempt to maintain a continuity for the look of their killer, as opposed to some other franchises that just have their killer randomly show up with a completely different look with zero explanation. (One of those other franchises will actually be this one in just a few movies.) The outfit that he goes with, the stolen laundry, would soon become the character's trademark look: faded blue jeans and an olive button-down shirt, with a white T-shirt underneath. His clothing would be some sort of variation on this look for the next several movies.

What's not really accounted for is Jason's shift in size, as he's massive in this movie. He went from being a pretty average-sized guy to being a hulking marauder in the space of a few hours. This is apparently an undocumented side effect of having a machete jammed into your shoulder, and it's surprising that this secret has not yet been exploited by the weightlifting industry. Of course, a new actor had taken on the role of the killer, this one assisted by some carefully placed padding to enhance his size. Richard Brooker, who played Jason in this film, was built slim, with a toned physique, and the decision was made to have Jason look more imposing. This would also be a pretty big shift for the character, and would shape his depiction going forward. He would no longer be a rather average-sized human being, but instead be a larger-than-life man-mountain.

As opposed to being set in a camp, this one actually takes place at Higgin's Haven, a vacation home spot that's also on the lake, and there's

Jason's (as portrayed by Richard Brooker) now-classic bald-headed look (*Friday the 13th Part III*, Paramount, 1982).

a new group of teenagers here. This one contains another odd continuity quirk with our lead character Chris and her flashback to two years ago. It seems that on a previous visit, she had a run-in with Jason in which he attacked her, although she doesn't remember what happened afterward and just woke up later in her own bed. The insinuation seems to be that Jason sexually assaulted her, but this is pretty contrary to everything that we already know about the character as well as anything that happens beyond this. The more likely scenario here is that she escaped the attack and was found by her parents and placed in her bed, thereby keeping the integrity of Mr. Voorhees being only a murderer and not a sex pest murderer, which is somehow worse. Even if you feel like it shouldn't be, it definitely is. Besides the weird implication of the scene, there's also a continuity issue in the fact that Jason appears to be wearing his clothing from this current film, instead of his outfit from the previous. I mean, it's expected that he would change his clothes and all, and wouldn't just be sporting that same old coverall set, but it's unusual that his flashback gear so closely matches the one that he had taken earlier in *this* movie. I suppose it's possible that that's his standard outfit, and he specifically stole that ensemble from the clothesline because it looked the closest to his personal style.

This is also the film that solidifies Jason's identity as the hockey-masked killer, as he dons it for the first time about three quarters of the way in. At the time, there was no indication that this aspect would become a defining aspect of the character. It's even obvious from the posters, which merely depict the killer as a shadowy figure, instead of hoisting the mask up there as a selling point. The idea of the mask was not one that was planned out, since it's never mentioned in the actual script, and stories of preproduction just contained references to a general mask, with no specific design chosen. The decision was made to just trade out the sack head for a different mask. It wasn't until they were prepping to shoot and doing lighting tests that Martin Jay Sadoff, the film's 3D supervisor, a big hockey fan, pulled out a goalie mask for them to try out. Miner fell in love with it, and it would soon become an iconic and integral part of the Voorhees mystique.

Again, the entire movie takes place over the course of two days. If *Part 2* began on a Thursday, it ended on Saturday morning. *Part III* picks up that Saturday and carries over into the next Sunday, with the ending of the movie occurring on Monday morning, as our Final Girl confronts Jason by the lake.

Again, another big element of the series lore develops here, as we are now given a Voorhees who is way more durable than we've seen before. Granted, Jason in *Part 2* took a machete to the shoulder and was able to survive, but it was that one blow that took him out of commission. In this one, in the finale, he's hung by his neck, which doesn't manage to kill him, and then has an axe firmly planted in his head. Even with this cranial contusion, he still lunges after Chris, trying to reach her for a little while longer. This unwillingness to just lie down and die would become even more accentuated as the series continued, eventually becoming more supernatural in nature, but even here, as Jason is still human, he is shown to be able to take a considerable amount of damage.

The film again ends on an ambiguous note, with Chris actually having two different dream sequences. The first involves a still-alive Jason coming after her as she rests in a boat on the lake, and the second mimics the first film as the decayed corpse of Pamela Voorhees rises up from the water to drag her under. This is notable because at no point in the movie is Chris told the story of Pamela, and she has no real reason to know about her, considering that she didn't really even have an awareness of who Jason was. This would seem to carry on the vaguely supernatural theme that threads in and out of the series, although it was more likely just a jump scare moment written in with little note of the logistics of how Chris would know Pam's story. But we're not here to talk about logistics, or else this book would be about half its current length.

An interesting detail is that originally, there was an intention to bring back the character of Ginny from the second film. The storyline would have revolved around a returning Amy Steel playing the character, recovering from her ordeal in a nearby psychiatric hospital. Jason would then seek her out and begin stalking anew, attacking the staff and other patients and forcing yet another face-off with her. When Steel turned the role down, reportedly due either to availability or an inability to meet her monetary demands, the script was then rewritten into its current form.

It should come as no shock when I say that the film was torn apart by critics, who once again noted that it was just more of the same, as if that weren't the reason people were going to see it in the first place. And they did go see it. Bolstered by the 3D gimmick, this one pulled in almost $37 million, a solid increase from the second part, even if it didn't quite hit the highs of the original.[3] It cost a little bit more, with a price tag of a little over $2 million, mainly due to the extra costs of the 3D equipment and imaging, but would still result in a very strong profit for the company, practically ensuring that the series would go on.

The fourth movie came two years later, in 1984, with *Friday the 13th: The Final Chapter*, which would be the last movie in the series. They promised that it would be and they put it right there in the title, and that's something you can't just go back on. If you call your film "the final chapter," it's essential that you don't make any more movies in the series after that. Steve Miner left the director's chair and Joseph Zito, who had previously put out the slasher flick *The Prowler*, stepped in.

It's of minor importance that Paramount decided to put out an entry called "The Final Chapter" right after making a substantial profit off of the third one. But it's also of note that *Part III* was originally intended to be the last one, the completion of the trilogy, marked as such by the fairly distinct death of Jason at the end. He had taken an axe to the head and we last saw his body, unmoving, on the floor of the barn. It's a pretty clear ending, but of course, the film made money. At this time, Frank Mancuso, Jr., Paramount producer, had become resentful of how popular the series had become and no longer wished for it to be associated with the studio. The big "but" at the end of that sentence was the fact that the third movie did so well. With that in mind, they chose to crank out one more entry, dubbing it "the final chapter" in an attempt to clearly finish the franchise.

Following the trend of the last film, this one again picks up where the last one left off, with Jason dead in a barn and the police on hand. This would place it still in 1985, and it's dark now, so it's hours later on that same Monday that the third film ended. Very shortly afterward, our villain proves himself to be very much alive, and returns to Crystal Lake, where a new group of teens awaits. It seems there's yet more houses on the lake, ones that we've never seen before and that Jason, in all his years in the area, never really bothered before.

Interestingly, as this group of kids, including a very young and unknown Crispin Glover, approaches the area, they pass a tombstone on the side of the road. The stone belongs to Pamela Voorhees, because when you're a mass murderer, I guess you get a random gravestone on the side of the road, not in a cemetery or anything. The inscription on it reads that she died in 1979, which upends the chronology of the series that we've established so far, but it's the first time in watching the films that a concrete date is given, so it becomes the starting point that we go from. If Pamela died in 1979, then that's when the first film is set, even though June 13 of that year did not fall on a Friday on our calendar. That being said, it's not entirely necessary for the days to line up in a fictional film universe in the way that they do with ours, so this is totally forgivable. It seems unlikely that whoever would have taken the time to make that gravestone would be incorrect about the year in which Pamela was killed, considering that they cared enough to actually make the thing. So, if the first film is set in 1979, that actually changes the following films as well. Since Paul stated that Pamela was killed five years ago in

Part 2, and *Part III* and *The Final Chapter* take place right afterward, that actually moves all three of those films into the year 1984. Oddly enough, that move shifts the fourth film into present day after the big time jump between *Parts 1* and *2*.

We also see a young Corey Feldman as one of the central protagonists of this one, as Tommy Jarvis, a special effects enthusiast at the lake with his mother and sister. In terms of series lore, this addition is a pretty important one, as Tommy will go on to become one of the few recurring protagonists in the entire run, as well as one of the few characters to return in another film and survive.

There's also an interesting wrinkle, from a timeline standpoint, with the introduction of a character named Rob. At first, he appears to be a hiker, up at the lake area for recreation, but is later revealed to be there on the hunt for Jason. It seems his sister was killed by Jason, and he believes him to still be on the loose and is attempting to track him down on his own. The issue with this is that he reveals his sister to be Sandra, a character from the second film. If this is true, that means his sister was murdered a mere four days ago or so, yet Rob has a stack of yellowed news articles about Jason and the killings. It seems unlikely that in the space of a few days, he was given the news of his sister's death, took care of everything involved with that, and did extensive research before heading out on his hunt. It was apparently noted as a mistake by the writers, claiming that they forgot that the three films took place essentially back to back, creating the time confusion.

Jason (Ted White): now featuring more wrinkles courtesy of Tom Savini (*Friday the 13th: The Final Chapter*, Paramount, 1984).

The film ends pretty spectacularly: Jason is unmasked and then killed by Tommy, who buries the killer's own machete into his face, causing him to fall onto it, pushing it about halfway through his head. In case that wasn't final enough, the young lad then takes the blade and hacks away about ten to fifteen times. The effect is easily one of the most memorable in the entire set of films, with a mixture of deceptive camera work and puppetry, the handiwork of a returning Tom Savini. The death was concocted to appear as permanent and inescapable as possible. It was easy to justify Jason surviving the end of *Part III*: perhaps the axe was slowed by the mask, and didn't quite penetrate his skull after all, and merely served to knock him unconscious. That death had enough plausible deniability to it that having him come back to life was a matter of writing "and then Jason got up." This was not so easy. With as much punishment as they had shown Voorhees able to absorb, there would be no way to say that he'd still be all right after having a blade basically cut half of his head off, and then be dealt a number of additional blows to boot. This death was meant to look completely final.

Because it was The Final Chapter.

Until it wasn't. Because Money.

The Final Chapter had an opening weekend of $11 million, the biggest of the series to date, and would go on to pull in $33 million in its run, against a budget of $2.6 million.[4] Although the initial debut of the film was stronger than normal, the cumulative run of the films continued to diminish, so it was clear that the series was losing steam. Due to his distaste for the franchise, and the decreasing returns, as *The Final Chapter* hit, Mancuso Jr. exited his role with the series. Immediately after, it became evident that although Mancuso intended to end the *Fridays*, Paramount had no such inclination.

So, just one year later, in 1985, the franchise continued with *Friday the 13th: A New Beginning*. Joe Zito didn't return and Danny Steinmann was tapped for the director's role—he had previously done the horror film *The Unseen*, as well as some work in the adult industry. This entry is infamous for its sleazier, dirtier feeling, as well as not featuring Jason, but for me, it's notorious for breaking the timeline.

Before we address that, we need to address the challenge handed to the screenwriters. They were faced with the unique dead end of writing a new chapter of a film franchise that revolved around a killer who had been pretty irrevocably taken out of commission. The fourth film had ended with the ominous shot of a seemingly now evil Tommy, so that was one avenue that could have been taken, but the decision was instead made to introduce a completely new killer while still also keeping Jason in the picture, through use of a disguise.

It starts off simply enough, with young Tommy at the grave of Jason Voorhees, so we're seemingly a short time after the end of the last film. But Corey Feldman was unable to return for the sequel outside of this scene, so a time jump was necessary. They had wanted Feldman to reprise the role of Tommy for the entire film and once again be the central protagonist, but the young actor was tied up doing *The Goonies* instead and was unavailable. Due to the hurried schedule of shooting the sequel, it was decided to recast the role with an older actor who could serve as a stronger opponent for Jason, as well as being a suspect in the killings.

So, after that brief setup is revealed to be a dream sequence, we bounce ahead an undetermined amount of time. Tommy is now much older and has been institutionalized due to the trauma of *The Final Chapter*. There's a bunch of interesting elements for our timeline in that he's being transferred to Pinehurst, a facility for troubled teens, so although John Shepherd, the actor taking over the role, was 24 years old at the time of shooting, we have to assume that Tommy is still a teenager. We are informed that he was 12 years old in the last movie, and there is a paper that documents his treatment that causes some issues of its own. There are several dates on there that show '82, as well as some that appear to read '76 or '78, all of which seem to be contradictory, as they seem to be stating that he was receiving those treatments during those time frames. If *The Final Chapter* was set in 1984, and Tommy is now still a teenager, the latest this film could be is in 1991, but judging from his appearance, it's clear that it's not just one or two years later. The latest treatment listed on the paperwork is from 1985, which would only be one year after the last film, which seems unlikely, but there's nothing saying that this is the complete paperwork. It may continue on another page or the back side of this one. In terms of the dates that are earlier than '84, it's possible that Tommy was receiving medical treatment prior to Jason's attack, for more standard childhood issues. It's also likely that this paper is just wrong. It's rife with misspellings, so it's easy to assume a clerical issue, considering that the word "docotrs" actually appears twice.

The actual amount of time between the two films is never made clear, and is not clarified in outside material, but the general consensus seems to be that this is five years later, and Tommy is now 17 years old, which is believable enough, considering 1980s films' propensity for casting people in their 30s as teenagers. If we go with that time frame, that would place this film in 1989, about four years ahead of when it was released. There is a visible calendar on a wall later in the film, but the year is obscured, although it does show that the film takes place in October.

Considering that it's set at the youth center, which is in Pinehurst, this becomes the first film in the series to not take place at Crystal Lake. It's insinuated that the area is near the lake, but this becomes our very first expansion into the world beyond.

The only other real issue that this film has in terms of series continuity is the mayor's statement that Jason Voorhees has been cremated and is no longer a concern, which obviously creates an issue for future entries. It was clear that they were trying to cement the notion that the original Jason was dead and buried, no longer a factor in the overall storyline, and writing this in would help to establish that. They had no idea at the time of writing that the genuine article would be forced into a reappearance not long afterward. A justification was actually written in later on that Jason's father himself paid off the county officials to fake the paperwork that his son was cremated, although that moment was never actually filmed. It could certainly be possible that the town just spread the story that the body had been burned in order to prevent people from seeking out his grave for morbid tourism, although that does raise a further question of why they wouldn't just go ahead and cremate him, instead of faking it. It could also be written off as an error of records, and a simple clerical mistake.

Beyond that, this doesn't play too much with any established timeline issues, considering that our villain is actually an imposter, an ambulance driver named Roy, and not Jason himself. This is probably the most controversial and divisive element of the film, since fans want to see Jason, not someone that looks exactly the same, doing the same thing, but wearing a mask. The idea is that Roy's son is a patient at the halfway home, a child he had abandoned years later. When that son is murdered by another patient, it drives him off the deep end and sends him on a murderous spree. He dresses as Voorhees in order to cover his tracks and throw off the local law enforcement.

There is a final confrontation that sees Tommy injured and Roy killed, finally revealing his identity. The ending actually sets up further entries in which Tommy would likely take up the mask and villain role, with him seemingly finally being corrupted. The thought was that Tommy could then take up the killer's identity and continue the series.

Again, the film was financially successful, but less so than the previous entries. Against a reduced budget of $2.2 million, *A New Beginning* ended its run with $22 million, a sharp drop-off from *The Final Chapter*.[5] This time, however, not only were critics negative about the film, but audiences were as well. The backlash of having an imposter take on the role of Jason rubbed fans the wrong way, and to this day remains one of the harshest critiques of the film. It became increasingly

The copycat killer is revealed to be Roy (Dick Wieand) (*Friday the 13th: A New Beginning,* Paramount, 1985).

clear that the star of the show was one Jason Voorhees, and the series could not continue without him, but he was extremely dead.

Until he wasn't.

A mere one year later, the saga continued with 1986's *Friday the 13th Part VI: Jason Lives.* As you can probably tell by the title, it features the return of our central villain. This represented the biggest challenge given to the writers yet. *A New Beginning* had once again ended with the potential to have Tommy Jarvis become the central antagonist, but the word from on high was that the series could not continue without the genuine article himself: Jason Voorhees. Whatever direction the new film would take, it would need to find a way to restore the killer from his grave. There was also a move to make the next entry softer, since the sleaze content of the prior chapter was another element that was roundly criticized. They wanted Jason back, but a kinder, gentler version.

And so, a new director was selected to take over and Tom McLoughlin took the reins, bringing an entirely new flavor to the series. McLoughlin was most known for a horror feature, 1983's *One Dark Knight,* but had several other scripts that were comedically oriented, which is what got him the job. If they wanted to take the edge off the franchise, what better way than to bring someone on board with more humorous sensibilities?

Tommy Jarvis also returns, but has again been recast, now played by *Return of the Living Dead*'s Thom Mathews, and it's clear that he didn't quite go evil, as was suggested by the last film. The first time we see him, he is driving Pam from the fifth film's truck, indicating that she is indeed alive, even though the last time she was seen, Tommy was advancing on her with a knife. Much, much later, some ancillary information provided for the official *Friday the 13th* video game would state that entire final sequence was merely a dream that Tommy was having.

The amount of time that has passed is unclear, but in the original script for the film, his age is stated to be 18, just one year older than the last film. Considering that we're once again set at a summer camp, right before the season begins, it's most likely around June or July. It's pretty likely that this is about six months or so after the last one, and between October 1989 and June 1990, Tommy turned 18 years old and was transferred to a more secure facility—only not so secure, since he's able to escape at the beginning.

This one's biggest contribution to the lore of the franchise is bringing Jason back from the dead, via a handy bolt of lightning, which changes him from a human killer to an unstoppable, undead murder zombie. This marks a major shift in the status quo for the character and makes blatant the supernatural overtones of the series for the first time. Whereas up until this point, Jason had been a strictly "human" force that is just difficult to kill, he's now firmly in the realm of fantasy. Oddly, this may be the version of the character that is now the most recognizable, with the average viewer probably envisioning the zombie-style character over his living variation.

Part 6's Jason (as portrayed by C.J. Graham) with his fresh-from-the-grave styling (*Friday the 13th Part VI: Jason Lives*, Paramount, 1986).

With this change of character comes a slight change of mannerisms, since he no longer runs, and simply walks after his victims from this point forward. Oddly, this trait begins in the previous film, with the Roy Jason walking after his victims, never seen running. It's unclear why he takes this tactic, although it makes a bit more film sense for the zombified version of the killer to take the easier pace. Again, the slow incarnation of the character is what is generally thought of when discussing Jason. Many filmgoers are surprised to discover that the earlier version would move at full speed, only seeing him as the slow killer he would evolve into.

A small bit of storyline that this entry adds is the renaming of the Crystal Lake area. It seems all the bad publicity over the past handful of years has tainted the community, which has finally decided to make a fresh start by calling the area Forest Green. Considering that *A New Beginning* didn't necessarily take place in the immediate Crystal Lake area, this change most likely occurred sometime over the past five years, between the confrontation in *The Final Chapter* and now.

One of the other major changes that occurs here is the studio-mandated shift in tone, as there are quite a few additional comedic moments sprinkled throughout. This shift is apparent from the beginning of the movie, as they replicate the James Bond gun barrel scene, except here it's Jason slashing the screen. There's a more lighthearted feel to a number of moments, including some comic relief paintball players. The kills of the movies are softer in general, with less emphasis on the gore aspects and more on the inventiveness.

Another thing that stands out here is the camp itself. For the first time in the series, we are shown the camp in full swing, with actual children attending. All of the previous films took place before the full season, with the counselors being trained, but here the session has begun, and kids of a variety of ages are present. There's even a scene near the ending in which Jason is in a room full of preteens and doesn't act, indicating that his penchant for murder does not include children. It's an interesting wrinkle, considering that he's previously been shown to be completely mindless when it comes to killing, with no particular issues with basically any victims. Perhaps he still views himself as that young camper and chooses to spare them, based upon some lost memory in what passes for Jason's brain.

The finale places Jason in a tough spot, chained up at the bottom of the lake, seemingly killed. Apparently, McLoughlin wanted to introduce a weakness to Jason, making him vulnerable on his "home soil," which seems to be the lake area, although this element isn't really conveyed within the actual film itself. It's a little confusing why he doesn't simply lift off the chain that is wrapped around his neck. He's seemingly incapacitated by taking an outboard motor to the neck, although it's not really clear why this action harms him when all others did not, except for the possibility that it's the home soil weakness in effect.

This marks the end of the "Tommy Jarvis trilogy," as that character now exits the franchise. He manages to survive intact, although possibly still on the run from the law. The character is never seen again in the series proper, although he shows up in several extended universe tales. He appears in a novel, several comic books, and the *Friday the 13th* video game, as well as several fan films that brought back actor Thom Mathews to reprise the role.

One other quick thing to note in terms of continuity between this film and the last is that the original plan was to have all the characters from *A New Beginning* return, including Pam and Reggie the Reckless, but when they decided to drop the "Tommy as the villain" storyline and bring Jason back, the actors' contracts were canceled. There do seem to be reports that an early version of the script did feature the character of Reggie, and that he was killed within the first 10 minutes, causing Shavar Ross to decline to return. I suppose it's possible that this void was then filled with the character of Allan instead, although that's merely speculation.

Also, as noted earlier, there was a scene written that would have ended the film on a cliffhanger. The unfilmed moment was to introduce Jason's father, merely called Mr. Voorhees, who would show up at the cemetery and meet with the caretaker there. Mr. V. would be informed of his son's resurrection, and the discussion would be had of his cremation being faked. The scene would end with the father giving an angry look, as we'd then see a shot of Jason's mask rising to the surface of the lake. It was never stated if his look indicated that he would end up assisting or opposing his son—that was left for future installments to carry off. However, this moment was never filmed, as the studio chose to have follow-ups solely focus on Jason and not get involved in more lore. Because of this, the scene was scrapped and the caretaker character was killed off in a reshoot, and although he's been featured in multiple extended universe tales, Jason's father never appears on-screen.

Unfortunately, the damage that had been done to the series' already tarnished reputation seemed to be insurmountable, and its box-office slide would continue. Although the film featured a revamped concept, more geared to the tastes of the audience, and the budget was slightly juiced up to $3 million, *Part VI: Jason Lives* didn't even crack $20 million when all was said and done. In its opening weekend, it brought in less than $7 million, losing out to *Aliens* in its third week of release.[6]

On the bright side, it did manage to beat out *Howard the Duck*, which debuted on the same date. So, if anyone asks you how popular the sixth *Friday the 13th* film was, you can say, "Well, it was slightly more successful than *Howard the Duck.*"

Two years later, in 1988, things continued with *Friday the 13th Part VII: The New Blood.* If *A New Beginning* was the film that broke the timeline, this is the one that steps on the pieces and grinds them into the ground.

In writing the film, the screenwriters were actually handed the clearest playing field so far. They were given a zombified killer that theoretically couldn't die, who was merely incapacitated at the bottom of a lake. They had no obligations to continue storylines or characters, and could go in any direction they wanted without having to jump through hoops to get there.

They only had one stipulation: make him fight Freddy.

Originally, the plan was for the series to cross over with the massively popular *Nightmare on Elm Street* series, a matchup that had fans chomping at the bit. At this point in time, though, Freddy was riding a massive wave of popularity, while Jason's limelight was fading, so New Line, the studio that produced the *Nightmare* films, held all the cards. When a suitable agreement couldn't be reached, the idea was dropped, and the tussle between the titans would go up on the shelf, where it would sit for over a decade.

The deal fell through, but the decision to have Jason go up against an opponent that could go toe to toe with him stuck. Screenwriter Daryl Haney came up with the idea of essentially doing "Jason vs. Carrie," with enough details changed to make the telekinetic teenage girl an entirely new (and copyright-free) character. They brought on John Carl Buechler, an established special effects artist who had branched into directed with the cult hits *Troll* and *Cellar Dweller*, to run the show.

The film opens with a shot of Jason, still chained up under the lake, so it's clear that we're set after the events of the last film. We're then introduced to Tina, a young girl who apparently lives nearby on the lake. It's a little unusual that there's a house right there, so close to where he's chained up, because the end of the last film established that the surrounding area is a summer camp, but I guess there's a couple of houses right on the other side of it. There is a calendar here, and although it doesn't show the year, it does show that it's October 13, very possibly just a few months after the ending of the last film, and it's October of 1990.

After introducing the notion that Tina has telekinetic powers and accidentally kills her dad, the movie then jumps ahead an undetermined amount of time, but Tina is clearly much older now. They never state exactly how much time has passed, but actress Lar Park Lincoln was 26 at the time of filming, although she's clearly meant to be much younger here. This is probably one of the most nebulous time frames, since the online community seems to be pretty set on it being a seven-year time gap, with the Tina from the beginning of the film being 10 years old and the rest of the film being Tina at 17. The film's director, John Carl Buechler, seems to dispute this, saying that Jason has been under the water for 10 years, accounting for his rotted out appearance. My solution actually fits both of those options, and also accounts for the houses being there. If the opening scene with young Tina takes place three years after the sixth film, it allows for them to close the camp at Forest Green, which is why we don't see it in the beginning of this one. In doing so, we're placing the prologue in October 1993, with the rest of the film occurring in 2000. It's an odd placement, because the clothing and cars don't really match the time period, but based on the film's timeline, the absolute earliest that this could be is 1997. Either way, it's not going to make sense, so just roll with it.

It should be noted that somewhere in this 10-year span, they reversed their decision about the name change and went back to calling the area Crystal Lake, as the name Forest Green is never used again. Near the end of the film, there is a calendar posted on the wall, but again, the year is obscured with the month being visible, and it's showing May, so we're setting this one in May 2000.

The time confusion aside, this one's actually pretty lined up with continuity. Buechler made sure to pay attention to past details, particularly the damage that Jason had received previously, making sure to include visible damage in places where he was attacked in the earlier films. As usual, the standard axe mark remains in the top corner of the hockey mask, but there is also a lower portion that has taken damage, a result of the outboard motor from the end of the last film. The side of his head also features a huge slash right along the side of it, and indication of the machete wound from the end of *The Final Chapter*. Also, since he's been at the bottom of the lake for a decade, his clothing is torn and tattered, nearly falling apart and covered with seaweed. Add to that several exposed bones, particularly on his back, due to the erosion from being in the water. This is clearly the most battle-damaged and beat-down looking Jason.

This would become known as one of the most imposing-looking Jasons of the series, due to the introduction of Kane Hodder to the role. The stuntman would go on to become the first actor to play the character more than once, and would play him in three subsequent entries. His portrayal of the character is noticeably different, as Jason acts angrier, more menacing in this entry. He's assisted by the ending of the movie, which features more screen time than usual for a maskless Jason, allowing for more facial emoting.

The film also kills one of the longest-running characters in the franchise so far: the hockey mask. Jason's hockey mask has been presumed to be the same one since the third film. The mask he takes from Shelly stays with him through the fourth movie, when he's killed, and somehow Tommy has it in his possession when reviving the menace. Now, whether the mask Tommy has is the genuine article or a reproduction that he's created is debatable, but it seems more likely that he wouldn't have brought it if it weren't the real deal, so Jason gets it back. It remains with him through that film and this one, until Tina uses her telekinesis to crack it in half, destroying it forever.

In terms of story continuity, the film would represent a return to form. Dropping some of the more "world building" aspects of the previous three films, this went back to the classic formula of "bunch of teenagers have a party at the lake and are killed off one by one." That is, until the telekinetic girl shows up.

The addition of Tina introduces yet another supernatural element to the lore, expanding the otherworldly aspects of the universe these characters live in. Outside of the more subtle spiritual notes of the early film, the creation of undead zombie Jason opened the door for more

Jason's (Kane Hodder) full-on zombie face revealed (*Friday the 13th Part VII: The New Blood*, Paramount, 1988).

fantastical details. Because of this, the concept of a teenage girl with superpowers doesn't necessarily feel out of place.

In the finale, Tina returns the killer to his watery grave. Jason is again trapped at the bottom of the lake, dragged down by the reanimated and yet not rotted corpse of Tina's long-dead father. It's complicated. So complicated, in fact, that it resulted in reshoots. Originally, the father was supposed to burst forth from beneath the docks, appearing as a rotted skeleton, the results of being underwater for 10 years. After pulling Jason down beneath the surface, he would then reappear in a spiritual form, saying goodbye to his daughter. The studio deemed this ending too confusing, so they ordered a reshoot with a mostly intact form of the father rising up to attack the killer. Why it was decided that a body sitting underwater for a decade and still looking exactly the same was *less* confusing is still a mystery.

That wasn't the only scene in the film that ended up being meddled with, since this entry received far more attention from the ratings board than usual. The MPAA, the committee that decides a film's rating upon release, slapped the film with the dreaded X rating due to the excessive violence. In order to receive an R rating, they had to go in and remove the vast majority of the violent effects, creating a virtually bloodless picture.

Upon release, it was once again savaged by the critics, with most pointing out its repetitive plot line and stock characters, many of them noting that the introduction of the Carrie-esque heroine isn't enough to distinguish the film.

Its performance at the theaters was disappointing as well. Although it didn't fare any worse than the previous entry, it didn't exactly perform much better. It did manage to hit number 1 in its debut weekend, a small achievement considering that there was no strong competition and the second-place movie was one that had been out for five weeks already. Overall, it raked in $19 million, about the same as *Part VI*.[7] That number is helped by the fact that it had a slightly reduced budget of $2.8 million, but comparatively, *Nightmare on Elm Street 4*, which would debut later that year, managed to bring in close to $50 million.

Because of this, Paramount was losing interest in the series, but it was still profitable enough for them to give it one more go. So in 1989, just one year later, the series had a change in scenery with *Friday the 13th Part VIII: Jason Takes Manhattan*, considered by many to be the worst film in the franchise. And that's saying something.

Buechler actually developed a follow-up to the previous film, writing a treatment which would see the character of Tina returning to once again battle Jason. It would be established that she was committed to an asylum after the events of the last one, and upon her release, would once again do battle with the maniac.

Paramount decided to go in another direction. They were frustrated with the series' sinking box office and realized that something drastic was needed to shake things up. Instead of bringing back Buechler, they instead brought on Rob Hedden to write and direct, marking his feature debut. He realized that the most important thing to do would be to get Jason away from Crystal Lake and bring him into an entirely new territory, so he developed two different concepts. The first would take place entirely on a cruise ship, while the second would take Jason into New York City. The studio actually approved both ideas, and the decision was made to combine them, placing the emphasis on the ship scenes to conserve the budget. Hedden also had an advantage in the fact that the previous film left Voorhees in an easily rectifiable situation. He was once again just at the bottom of the lake, with no extremely extenuating circumstances preventing him from being revived.

Because of that, it kicks off with our villain exactly where we left him, at the bottom of the lake with a dock on top of him, but then things start to get confusing as far as continuity goes. There is a small luxury liner on the lake, populated with a pair of obligatory horny teenagers. This is sort of an issue because in almost every other appearance of the lake, it's fairly small. The only boats we've seen on the lake have been little ones, mostly rafts, surely not 25-foot cabin cruisers. Regardless, there's one there now, and its anchor manages to catch onto some electrical wires and connect them to Jason somehow, which brings him back to life. Most likely, this is carrying forward with the plot element introduced in *Part VI* with the bolt of lightning, insinuating that Jason is now somehow similar to Frankenstein in the sense that he can be revived through electricity.

With his mask destroyed in the previous film, this one had to come up with a reason for him to have it again, so they chose the most logical way to go. There's just another hockey mask on the boat. Really. The previously mentioned horny teen decides to play a prank on his girlfriend and brings along a Jason-inspired mask to do so, and it's an exact reproduction, down to the battle damage in the upper region from the axe blow in *Part III*. I suppose the implication is that the Jason legend is well known enough for them to market him, which is slightly believable considering that they've shown that his exploits have been widely reported, although one would think his level of notoriety would have people a little more concerned about the spot where his body was reported to be.

The time frame between the two movies is never really stated, but the only aspect that gives any sort of hint is the fact that the young man in the beginning didn't really talk about the Jason killings as if they were something that happened recently, so it's not hard to assume that there's been some sort of time gap between this film and the last one. Considering that the events of *Part VII* would have to have made at least some sort of news, it's likely a couple of years, so if we give it a two-year push, that would set this one in 2002. There's a bit of an issue in that the same guy also tells the story of Jason and says that he drowned 30 years ago, which would have been in the '70s, which is of course pretty incorrect, but he's just a guy telling a story, so it's expected that he'd get elements wrong. Oddly enough, the 30-year thing actually does work if you assume that the film is set in real time, but the timelines they give in the movies make that extremely impossible given the huge jumps.

If those were the only issues with continuity with the film, then it'd be par for the course with the rest of them, but this one goes above and beyond with some additional issues. First of all, we're suddenly told that there's a high school by the lake, with an entire graduating class of students. Now, every other time they've shown the surrounding areas of the lake, it's been a pretty backwater town and very few young people have been shown. You could assume, however, that we haven't really seen the little town area in about 20 years or so, considering the gaps in time that we've been shown, and it's possible that in that stretch, a school was built and filled with local kids, because, you know, as a parent, you want your kid to attend the school near the site of all the murders. One thing to note is that the school teens have gathered for a graduation cruise, which would insinuate that this is set around the spring time, possibly in May or June of '02.

But then there's the big one. The biggest point of confusion of this entry: the revelation that it appears as if you can fit an entire cruise ship on Crystal Lake, and that it leads out into the ocean. Again, just to point out that in every previous appearance, it's been a small rural lake, so this is a pretty big surprise. At first, it seems as if there's the possibility that this isn't actually Crystal Lake, and is simply another nearby body of water, a much larger one, separate from the lake area seen in the introduction. But then the boat from the beginning comes floating along, complete with the dead teenagers on board and Jason in tow, which confirms that we are looking at the same body of water. The filmmakers again have noted that it was a mistake that was made, but honestly, it's only the first of what can be considered a feature-length string of mistakes. It can possibly be theorized that it actually is a separate body of water, separated by a small waterway, like a canal, that links them together. Perhaps the boat cruised down that waterway and joined up with the larger one.

Another one of those mistakes appears to be the design of young Mr. Voorhees. There are several psychic flashbacks that our Final Girl, Remy, witnesses of a child Jason, seemingly warning her of danger. She had also apparently had a run-in with him in the lake itself when she was younger, which would be an odd thing if the series is running with the notion that Jason never actually drowned in the lake, and instead survived and was living in the woods. Again, judging from her age in the flashback, Remy's earlier encounter would have occurred around ten years earlier or so, a time period in which Jason actually would have been in the lake, but not as a child. Keep in mind that if this is indeed taking place around 2000 or so, Jason would be in his 50s. For her to have encountered a ghost child Jason, it would have to have over 40 years earlier. Remy's graduating high school, and I'm assuming she wasn't held back that much. Instead, that setting would place her meeting around the era of *Part VI*'s ending, and a much older Jason would instead be chained up under the water. It's suggested by this, then, that the premonition child is merely an imagined vision of him, which is possibly why his facial structure appears to change. In some appearances, he's deformed still, and in others, his face is normal, suggesting a supernatural or hallucinatory nature to him. Perhaps this is the last vestige of his humanity, trapped within the water through whatever supernatural occurrences have led to all of this.

Jason Takes Manhattan is most notorious for the character not even really taking Manhattan—more like poking his head into it. The bulk of the runtime takes place on the cruise ship, with the cast only arriving in the city in the film's last twenty minutes or so, and even then, the city of Vancouver fills in for New York for most of that. There are a few shots of Times Square, however, and they do show several posters for movies and shows that ran in 1989, but clearly in this version of things, those came out much later, since there would be no way to reconcile this film taking place in 1989, just 10 years after Pamela's reported death, considering that the series' time frame includes a five-year jump to the second movie, another five-year jump in the fifth, and no less than seven-year jump in the seventh.

There's another big gap in continuity with the overall appearance of Jason. Sometime between this film and the last one, someone apparently swam down in the lake and changed his outfit. Although the film explains why his mask no longer has some of the damage, the same cannot be said about his clothing. Instead of the tattered olive green button-down shirt and torn up greenish pants, he's now sporting a bluish-toned button-down shirt that's remarkably intact. His pants also no longer feature tons of rips all over them, although they do appear to

Prepare to be disappointed with Jason's (as portrayed by Kane Hodder) pumpkin-face look (*Friday the 13th Part VIII: Jason Takes Manhattan*, Paramount, 1989).

again be similar in color, but his clothing is now constantly slimy and wet.

As stated earlier, Kane Hodder returns in the role of the killer, becoming the first actor to reprise the role. Because of this, there's a continuity to the movements and mannerisms to the character.

This film also introduces one of the more confusing aspects of Jason lore: his teleportation abilities. Throughout the films up until this point, there have been several instances where our killer manages to end up ahead of his victims. However, most of these seem plausible, with Jason taking advantage of the environment to maneuver around his prey and head them off at the pass. In this film, there's no mistaking it: Jason teleports. In at least three instances, we see him firmly planted in place as someone runs away from him, only for him to pop up ahead of them. In one of the occurrences, he's on a city street and then somehow magically appears on the second floor of a building. This superpower is never really explained, and it's presumed that it's just a filmmaking trick, but from a film standpoint, it's extremely odd, since there's no other way to explain how it happens outside of magical translocation. Interestingly, this trait was picked up in the newest video game and depicted as an actual ability, instead of an implied one.

The finale takes place in the sewer system, where we get the biggest shoulder shrug of all when it's revealed that every night at midnight, the sewers are flooded with toxic waste. No reason is ever given as to where all the waste is coming from, why there is so much of it, and where it eventually goes. It's perhaps one of the most confusing plot points in the entire series and I'm honestly not sure if it's more or less believable than a man brought back from the dead after being struck by lightning.

This scene also brings up another quirk of continuity, as Jason's face appears altered once again. Practically every time the mask comes off, the look of the character is different, but *Part VII* gave us a pretty definitive look. In this one, he instead has a sort of wilted pumpkin look, and is pretty disappointing. It's fairly explainable, though, since we don't see the face until after Remy has hit him with a splash of the toxic waste that just so happens to litter the sewers of New York.

Our big bad is caught in the waste flood, at which point he is then transformed back into his child form, minus the deformities. It's possibly the most confusing death of the character in all of the films, and doesn't really jibe with the tone of the series so far. There are several possible interpretations as to what this scene even means. The first is that it's literal, and that the waste has literally somehow mutated Jason back into his childlike form, not only resetting him to starting point, but actually fixing his physical maladies. The second is that it's somehow mystical, and that the waste essentially burned away the evil that was in possession of his body, leaving behind only the pure form of Jason. The final option is that it's not real, and we are only seeing the image of young Jason through Remy's eyes, and that it is not to be taken literally. Not only had she previously been seeing premonitions of the boy, but earlier she had forcibly been injected with drugs, and we may be being shown her hallucinated vision.

Any way you want to slice it, it was a very difficult ending to move forward from. It seems that after debating being done with the franchise for several movies, Paramount was finally pulling the trigger on stepping away from it. They wanted the denouement to double as an actual ending for the series, even if they didn't quite bill it as such, much as they did with *Part III*. Obviously, they didn't promote it as being the final chapter again, since they wanted to keep the option open of doing more, should *Part VIII* return the box office numbers to their former glory. As such, it could be viewed as the end of this particular run of films. Should the viewer choose to have this be the final fate of Jason, the option is there.

Even though the ticket sales had been slumping, and the last film benefited slightly from a reduced budget, they increased the amount spent on this one, upping it to $5 million dollars, the most expensive entry in the series so far. This was further compounded by a stronger marketing campaign, stressing the New York City aspect of the film.

They even had Hodder appear in character on *The Arsenio Hall Show*, a popular talk show at the time, to promote the film. In fact, the film's marketing got the studio into a bit of hot water, since they were sued by the state of New York for featuring their trademarked "I Heart NY" campaign, with Jason slashing his way through it. A complaint was filed, so Paramount ultimately recalled the campaign and replaced it with a much simpler shot of Jason above the New York skyline.

Unfortunately, that was all for naught, since the film was a huge box-office disappointment. In its opening weekend, it placed fifth overall, against heavy competition, including the debut of *Turner and Hooch* and summer heavyweights *Lethal Weapon 2* and *Batman*. And even though its initial numbers brought in $6 million, a comparable opening to several of the previous entries, it would only go on to accumulate $14 million over its run, a pretty large drop-off. It remains to this date the lowest-grossing film in the entire franchise.[8] Bear in mind that it also faced some strong horror competition that year, sharing the spotlight with *Nightmare on Elm Street 5* and *Halloween 5*.

Reception of the film was mostly negative, as well, with a large number of the reviews focusing on the fact that a movie called *Jason Takes Manhattan* largely takes place on a cruise ship. Oddly enough, esteemed film critic Leonard Maltin gave the film a slightly more favorable review than usual, claiming it was the best of the entire series and noting that it took the franchise in a bold direction.[9]

Regardless of what Maltin said, the writing was on the wall for the series. Paramount, who had been wanting to distance themselves from the franchise for the better part of a decade, decided to finally cut ties with it. They sold off the rights to New Line Cinemas, which had also been producing the *Nightmare on Elm Street* films, allowing them to take the reins of the series. And they would, leading to a couple of the most unusual takes on the character of Jason to date.

New Line pulled off an impressive feat by lining up Sean S. Cunningham, director of the original film, to return in a producer role. It would be his first involvement with the series since the first film, and he wanted to start strong by once again suggesting that Jason take on Freddy Krueger. However, the studio wanted to put that on the back burner for the moment and instead focus on a solo tale for their first foray. They asked him to develop an entirely original concept.

The screenwriters had several difficult hurdles to jump in their journey to bridge the gap between the previous *Friday the 13th* films and the new one. First of all, there were issues with rights, since the deal with Paramount was pretty limited. They weren't really given license to include characters from the previous entries, and it's debatable how much of the earlier situations were even allowed to be discussed. So they couldn't bring back Remy to follow up from the last one, assuming that was something they would even want to do. There were plans to have Tommy Jarvis return to the action, but were then informed they weren't allowed to do so, and the character was altered to one who would eventually be known as Steven Freeman. The earliest form of the script would curiously ignore *Part VIII: Jason Takes Manhattan* entirely, and instead pick up where things were left off at the end of *Part VII.* Jason would still be at the bottom of the lake, incapacitated by Tina, and would be dredged up and taken to a lab for an autopsy. While there, he would awake, only to see his heart being torn out by the coroner, who would then eat it and gain his powers. This would render Jason powerless and the mystery man would then continue his murderous spree. The man would then be revealed to be Elias Voorhees, a name that has since been ascribed to Jason's father, but this script seems to establish it as a previously unmentioned brother. Although this character was eventually dumped, elements of this draft would play a part in the finished product. Apparently, another early version of the script took things in the completely opposite direction of *Part VIII*, at least geographically. There was a version in which Jason went to Los Angeles and got in the middle of a gang war, killing off members of both sides until they would have to come together to face their mutual foe. This concept was also set aside, possibly due to Cunningham's distaste for the look of Jason. It seems that the producer never really cared for the hockey-masked styling of the villain and wanted to see it downplayed in this new entry, so having the character loose in LA wouldn't really work for that.

Adam Marcus, a protege of Cunningham, was selected to take on the project, his first feature film at the young age of 23. It was his idea to take the series as far away from what was previously established as possible, and break entirely new ground for the franchise.

The working title of the film was *Friday the 13th Part 9: The Dark Heart of Jason Voorhees*, but another minor detail of the deal with Paramount was their inability to use the title of *Friday the 13th.* As a result of that, the new film was dubbed *Jason Goes to Hell: The Final Friday.* That's right. They were going with the whole "final chapter" move once again. Not sure why New Line went with the tactic of ending the franchise with their first crack at the rights, but after I start talking about some of the choices made in the movie itself, this will seem to be the least questionable.

Because of the rights transition, it took four years between the eighth and ninth films, and *The Final Friday* wouldn't arrive until 1993, the longest gap between entries in the series so far. And if someone doesn't pick *Jason Takes Manhattan* as their least favorite, then most likely they're going with this one. It's a film that proudly flips the finger at any notion of continuity and upends the entire apple cart, which was fairly easy, to be honest, considering how beat up the cart was already. It could probably be said that the apple cart was already on the edge of a cliff with one wheel dangling over the edge, the contents having gone bad a long time ago.

The opening of the film pays tribute to the entire series so far, by playing into all of the tropes that have been established, giving us a young lady alone in a cabin by Crystal Lake attacked by Jason, who is no longer a child. No explanation is given for his transformation back into his full grown self, and the toxic waste ending of the previous film is ignored. Whether this lack of explanation can be attributed to not having the rights to the previous entry, or just a disinterest in addressing it, considering how poorly received that the situation had been, is unknown, but judging from the previous draft's picking up after the ending of *Part VII*, it seems clear that they had an interest in ignoring the eighth film. If the viewer is interested in making the continuity work between entries, it can be assumed that the change was just Remy's hallucination, but it can also be discarded as being a temporary change. Considering Jason's appearance in this one, a bloated, malignant-mass-covered man whose hockey mask is not partially embedded into the skin of his face, it's more likely that we're seeing him post–sludge bath. It clearly had an effect on him, warping his form even

Jason (Kane Hodder) shows up with his mask now embedded in his face (*Jason Goes to Hell: The Final Friday*, **New Line, 1993**).

more, and when he put the mask back on, it buried itself further into his flesh. In a callback to the second film, he also now has some long tufts of hair.

Kane Hodder returned to the role, marking his third outing as the madman, so there was a bit of consistency with his portrayal, although almost everything else about his look was different. His skin had less of a zombified look and more of a mutated one—again, possibly a side effect of the toxic waste. On an interesting note, this is actually the first film to not show what is underneath the mask, due to it being permanently fused onto his face. Over the years, people have theorized about what his mug would look like under there, with the video game finally visualizing it, showing a more skeletal look than before. Another tiny confusing snarl is the weathered portion on the lower region of the mask, the point of damage received at the end of *VI* and visible in *VII*. This was not seen in *Part VIII*, due to it being a new mask, but the mask that showed it was destroyed. This could hint at the movie ignoring the events of *Part VII* as well, or it could again be damage caused by the toxic waste, and just more wear and tear to match the rest of it.

In this one's intro, the woman at the cabin is shown to be a trap, and there's a SWAT team there to destroy Jason, which they do, blowing him into smithereens. It can be assumed that this is not too long after *Part VIII*, since it is probable that the killer's appearance in the thick of New York City caused a bit of media attention. You would have to figure that to be the straw that broke the camel's back in this situation, causing law enforcement to finally put an end to the killing sprees. Allowing for some time for Jason to return to his home base, the stories of the New York attacks to spread, and for the enforcement teams to get their plan together, a year or so seems likely. It's possible that it's later in the same year, but considering that it appears to once again be the beginning of the summer season, I think it's more likely to be around that time in the following year, so around June 2003, allowing some time for the big fella to grow out those long, lovely locks.

Since Jason is completely blown to pieces here, it seems as if *The Final Friday* is going to be shorter than you'd think, but then it introduces the biggest continuity curveball in the series to date. It's revealed that Jason's evil can spread from person to person, and he can take them over, possessing their bodies and using them to continue killing. Even the continuity for this isn't consistent, since in the beginning of the film, the chain is started when the coroner taking care of the body bites into the blackened heart of it, but then later on, it's a sort of worm demon thing that spreads from mouth to mouth, a la the film *The Hidden*. The worm thing is explained to be Jason's true form that he reverts to when his body is destroyed, although it's never mentioned why it didn't appear after his death at the end of Part 4, *The Final Chapter*. It would seem that this storyline takes the Elias draft further, and instead of making a single person take on the evil of Jason, it becomes a chain of people, a la the film *The Hidden*. This would allow them to keep the central focus of the storyline as Jason Voorhees being the villain, yet eliminate the hockey mask element that Cunningham so hated. It also creates an element of uncertainty as to the killer's identity, since it could theoretically become anyone ... a la the film *The Hidden*. Marcus, who came up with the body-swapping concept, acknowledges that the two conceits are remarkably similar, but states that he had not seen the earlier film before proposing his story.

There are several other elements that defy the established storyline, prompting some fans to consider this film to be a separate universe, not actually a part of the same timeline as the previous eight films. One of these elements is the introduction of a character named Creighton Duke. Duke is a bounty hunter who has somehow had a previous run-in with Jason, if not multiple encounters, and seems to know quite a lot about the villain's history, abilities, and family history. He's never been seen before in the franchise, so his knowledge is a bit suspect, and the only time frame in which it would be possible for him to have that encounter would probably be before the second film. It's plausible that he could have met up with Jason at some point in the space between the eighth film and this one, but it does seem as if he insinuates that their history is a little more long-term. Some fans have theorized that Duke was possibly intended to be Tommy Jarvis, given his talk of multiple encounters and extensive knowledge, but there doesn't seem to be anything to support that, and it seems unlikely considering it's been acknowledged that the character of Steven started out as Jarvis, so it would be unusual to have another sort of avatar for the character here.

The other new aspect that this movie introduces is Jason's extended family. After being destroyed, it's revealed that the only way for him to return to his previous form is to be reborn through the body of a Voorhees. Luckily, one exists, and we learn that Jason has not only a sister, but a niece and grandniece. They've changed their names to avoid being lumped in with their murderous relatives, but apparently Elias Voorhees had another offspring. This, by proxy, gives us more information about Jason's father than we've had so far. Since Diana is clearly younger than Jason would have been were he not a reanimated corpse, she had to have been born after him. That would sort of imply that Elias either left Pamela, or had an affair that produced an illegitimate daughter.

Although Diana's age isn't given, actor Erin Gray was actually born just a few years after Jason's fictional birthday, so an assumption can be made that he left Pam due either to her insanity or to the difficulty of raising a handicapped child.

The family element creates another new plot point for the series, in that it's revealed that a Voorhees family member can destroy Jason's evil once and for all, using a special dagger. This is a pretty drastic change for the character and the overall lore of the series. There's never been a sort of mystical kryptonite before. All of the previous methods of killing Jason have been more tactile and based in physicality, so the inclusion of a supernatural Achilles heel seems a little out of place. That being said, it doesn't feel any more or less out of place than any of the other elements added in this entry.

During the finale, the supernatural elements go into overdrive, as it's then revealed that Jason can be reborn into his true form through a member of his own family. To this end, he's been stalking his niece, Jessica, and her daughter, Stephanie. After being unable to get his hands on either one, the body that he's in becomes drastically damaged.

On a side note, the film raises a very important question in the last act, one that sort of defies its own logic, such as it is. At one point, an unseen character is taken over by the Jason worm, but the audience isn't shown who. A little later, there is a moment in which two characters are trying to get to Jessica, and it's unclear which of them has been taken over. Both suspects are shown talking, using a regular voice and demeanor to try to convince her that the other one is possessed. However, every single other person that has been under the sway of the evil has been as mute as Jason always has been, incapable of using subterfuge to their advantage and just operating under the standard Voorhees tactic of advance and attack. The fact that in this one instance he suddenly decides to communicate vocally seems to indicate that he has always been capable of this, or at least as long as he's been body-hopping. That makes it pretty unclear, then, why he hasn't chosen to use this technique up until now. It would seem that he could've achieved his goals a lot quicker by pretending to not be possessed like this, instead of just storming in everywhere. It also indicates that Jason does possess a rudimentary intelligence and has reasoned thought, even if it's literally only evident in this single scene.

Anyway, after that body is destroyed, the worm thing is forced out. It manages to find the body of Jason's half-sister in the basement, which it then uses to return to his former self. The worm does this by shimmying up the vagina of Diana Kimble, a shot that Erin Gray was unaware of. She was horrified at its inclusion. Marcus claims this shot was not his idea, and was instead a decision of the production team. After being reborn, Jason reappears in his previous form, clothing and all, because magic.

Another massive supernatural aspect is introduced during the final fight, as Jessica uses the dagger and plunges it directly into Jason's chest. This calls up demons from hell to claim him and pull him down into the underworld, ending the series for the second time.

Then, of course, the ending that everyone had been waiting for happens. Freddy Krueger's glove erupts from the ground to drag down Jason's mask, hinting at a showdown between the two terror titans. As a minor bit of trivia, Freddy's hand in this shot was played by Kane Hodder himself, giving him the opportunity to claim to be the only actor to portray both icons. For years, fans had been waiting for this, and it was finally possible due to New Line having the rights to both characters. It didn't matter that they referred to this film as the last one—this final shot told the fans there was bound to be more, and that more would include the showdown between the terror titans. Unfortunately, the project was a little easier said than done, and audiences would have to wait a little over a decade to see it come to fruition.

One quick aside: there's also another franchise crossover in the film, as the Necronomicon from the *Evil Dead* series makes a brief cameo at the Voorhees house. Again, it's unsaid in the film, but can be inferred that they were trying to say that two universes are connected, and that Pamela Voorhees used the cursed tome to either restore her son to life after drowning or imbue him with supernatural abilities in order to defy death. In fact, Marcus has admitted that this was his actual intention, and that Jason was intended to be a Deadite, one of the demons from the other franchise. That would seem to state that the creature that we've been following has never really been Jason, just a creature from hell called by the Necronomicon inhabiting his form.

New Line played it safe with the budget, keeping it at $3 million, which was a drop from the previous entry, but slightly higher than any of the others. Even though it had a decent opening weekend, delivering $7.5 million, it would only go on to total just under $16 million in its run.[10] This made it the second to lowest haul of the series, only slightly topping *Part VIII*, and was considered a disappointment once again. As noted earlier, the reaction was pretty sour, with many fans referring to it as the worst in the series, and a large contingent declaring that it wasn't actually canon, taking place outside the main continuity. Some say that since it is now under a different production umbrella, it can be viewed as a soft reboot.

I think it was pretty clear to everyone involved that *The Final*

Friday was never actually intended to be the last one. But it would seem for a while as if New Line were keeping their promise, and that Jason would actually just stay there, in hell. In fact, it became the only *Friday* film to be released in the '90s. The intention was to follow up on that by making good on the promise of *The Final Friday*'s finale and having the much ballyhooed Voorhees vs. Krueger showdown, but that movie had a much longer road to travel.

Over the next handful of years, that film would run the gauntlet with script concepts and revisions, with dozens of revisions and restarts. A number of directors would be either attached or approached by the studio, including Peter Jackson and Rob Zombie, both of whom would turn it down. Drafts included Tommy Jarvis and Neil Gordon, although the decision was ultimately made to focus on new characters, free of any existing continuity. Scripts would be rejected over and over again, with a number of screenwriters taking a crack at it, but nothing ever coming to fruition.

The frustration of nothing happening with the property got to be too great, and Sean S. Cunningham became concerned that audiences would lose interest in the property, so he moved to get another movie in the can. He brought on Todd Farmer to handle the script duties, and an assortment of ideas were thrown about, but in the spirit of Exquisite Corpse, there were multiple challenges to address from the ending of the previous entry. They had to address having Jason in hell, banished forever, and take care of the mention of Freddy's glove, knowing that a crossover film was still in the making. The decision was made to set the film in the future, after the events of the inevitable *FvJ* film, and they would take the character to space.

The idea of moving a horror franchise to space wasn't new. John Carpenter had suggested it as a setting for the sixth *Halloween* film. *Hellraiser* had already gone there. Hell, even the *Critters* had been there. Honestly, by the time this all happened, the premise was considered a punchline. "When you have no other ideas, send your villain to space." But they went ahead and did it anyway with 2002's *Jason X*, so called because, again, they did not have the rights to the *Friday the 13th* name.

In terms of continuity, it doesn't really link up to anything that came before it, and seemingly ignores quite a bit. Directed by the director of *The Horror Show*, the late Jim Isaac, this starts off in a rather unique place: with Jason in captivity. It seems at some point, they were able to capture him and imprison him, keeping him chained up 24/7. He escapes, of course, and ends up being cryogenically frozen, along with an obligatory Final Girl.

Due to their not wanting to contradict whatever would be planned for the Freddy matchup, they skip over any dangling threads left by the last one. It's never stated how he was caught, or how he even escaped hell. He's just there, and has been for some time.

Once again, Jason's appearance has changed pretty dramatically. He's distinctly less zombified, and his mask no longer appears to be infused into his face. The mask appears to be the same one, considering it still has the axe notch in the upper portion, but it is missing any of the other deterioration that occurred in the other films. Considering that it has a slightly different shape and now features a sort of nose protrusion, it's likely that this is a new mask. When you take into account that Jason masks appear to be marketed with the upper notch, as seen in *Part VIII*, this is probably another new mask. Not that they had the foresight, but this is also a different mask than we will see in *Freddy vs. Jason*. At one point in the film, we see his face without the mask, and he again sports a new design, and has started growing hair on his head, in what appears to be sort of a military-style crew cut, although it's in random patches. There's a new wrinkle, as a military man, played by legendary director David Cronenberg, states that the big J has regenerative abilities, like a healing factor. This can explain why he's been able to heal up from the damage that he's received over the course of the series, as well as why he looks less like a rotted-out corpse. It could even be theorized that this works retroactively, and Jason has always been this way. His death at the end of the fourth movie may have been an extremely difficult round of damage to recover from, and the regeneration may have been working

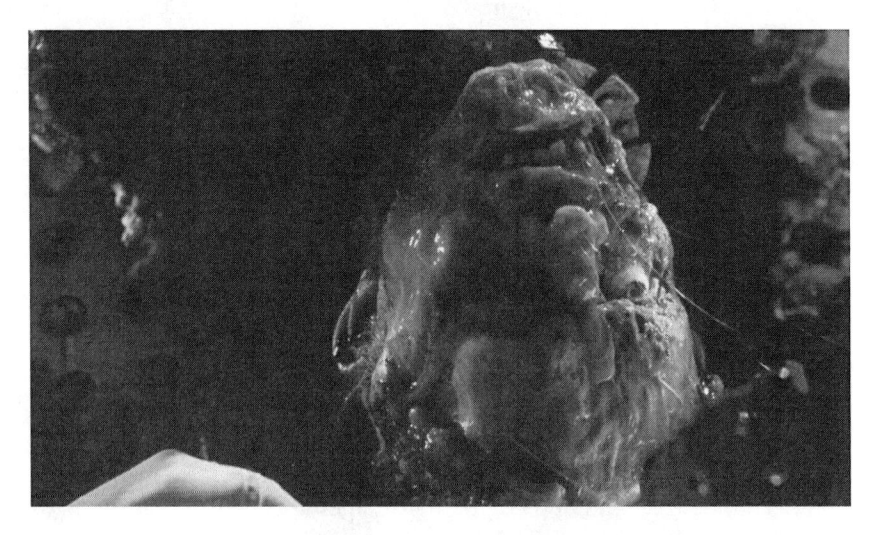

A look under the mask, showing Jason's (Kane Hodder) slightly more intact face (*Jason X*, New Line, 2001).

while he was buried. Perhaps the bolt of lightning served to jump-start him, as opposed to fully bringing him back.

In the far future, Jason and his victim are thawed out, and it's revealed that the cryo chamber they were kept in was from 2010, giving us a placement for the opening segment of the film. Oddly, they both state that the future year is 4.55 centuries and also say that it's 2455, though 4.55 centuries from 2010 would actually be 2465, so it's clearly an error, even though it's a robotic character that states the numbers. Given that two separate people then confirm the 2465 number, it would appear as if that number is correct, even if I would be more inclined to take the word of the living computer. Apparently, her human programmer didn't do a good job with her mathematical coding. There's also mention of previous attempts at executing Jason, and it's said that the first try was in 2008, so we know that he was apprehended at some point before then, giving a five-year gap between the movies for him to escape hell and be captured.

Three-quarters of the way through the film, after killing off most of the future ship's crew, Jason is killed by the robot character, who blows off his arms, legs, and eventually half of his head. Fortunately for him, his body lands on a nanotech surgery tool, which restores his body and turns him into a cyborg Uber-Jason. He now sports a metal arm and leg, along with a fancy chrome-looking mask and bright red eyes. This version of Jason appears to be stronger than before, able to tear through solid steel with his bare hands, and is capable of surviving in space with no equipment. Oddly, considering that this machine appears to be able

Everyone's favorite: Uber Jason (Kane Hodder) (*Jason X*, New Line, 2001).

to do some pretty drastic restoration of body parts, it's not really utilized by the other characters of the film. Seems like that would have come in handy against a villain that has a habit of chopping off body parts.

In a small nod to continuity, there's a scene in which the survivors are trying to throw Jason off their trail, and they do so by activating a hologram chamber. It creates an illusion of Crystal Lake, circa the '80s, and features a pair of classic, topless, horny coeds.

Since the only things that came out after *Jason X* were *Freddy vs. Jason* and the remake, and neither one picks up this story where it leaves off, in theory, this is where this version of Jason ends up. The last time we see him he is flying through space, headed down to an Earth-like planet, possibly burning up in the atmosphere, but more likely landing, healing up, and beginning to kill again. Like the two movies before it, it's perfectly acceptable to view it as a sort of end to the franchise, and also possible to view it as its own universe, separate from canon.

Jason X was shot in 2000, but had a string of issues during filming and beyond. To start with, there were pretty massive creative differences between James Isaac, the film's director, and the producers. After the film was complete, there was a shakeup in management at New Line, and the new regime didn't quite care for the finished product, and so they sat on it. Ironically, this one received the least amount of criticism from the MPAA, requiring minimal cuts in order to get an R rating. It remained up on a shelf for a while, but was released in Germany in July 2001 and then Spain that November. Its US release would take an additional five months, and it wasn't until April 2002 that it would grace American screens. This was the early days of widespread internet piracy, and a version of the film would leak online, where it would become one of the top downloaded torrents for several months. Very possibly as a result of this, when it eventually did debut in theaters, ticket sales were once again disappointing.

As opposed to the previous film, New Line did not play it safe here, increasing the budget to a lofty $11 million, although some have it reported as high as $14 million. This was a significantly higher price tag than any of the previous entries, more than doubling the budget of *Part VIII*. As such, the stakes were much higher for the film to perform well. To the surprise of no one who was watching the performance of the previous four films, it didn't. The opening weekend sputtered out at a mere $6.5 million, ending up behind *The Scorpion King*'s second weekend and *Changing Lanes*' third. After a run of a few weeks, it only managed to muster up a take of about $17 million worldwide, which was a slight improvement over the previous two films, but only just.[11] It's hard to quantify exactly how much of this was due to the film's online leak and how many of those downloaders would have been potential ticket buyers, but it's easy to see that the number would have to be at least somewhat meaningful.

Ultimately, the film was always intended as a stopgap measure, and *Jason X*'s missteps wouldn't affect the next step on the journey, the long promised *Freddy vs. Jason.*

The face-off had been long gestating, and it's estimated that New Line spent around $6 million on the script development alone. Finally, the writing task was handed to newcomers Mark Swift and Damian Shannon, who would utilize elements from the previous drafts, but also bring a new perspective to the storyline.

It was directed by Ronny Yu, who had previously made his name overseas with a series of stylistic Hong Kong horror films, as well as making a splash in the US with *Bride of Chucky*, proving that he was capable of bringing a fresh take to franchises previously thought stale. Fans were immediately split on his contributions, since with his intention to make Jason the more sympathetic of the two monsters, more in line with a Frankenstein's Monster kind of character, it was decided not to have fan favorite Kane Hodder return to the role.

For continuity, it actually does manage to fit in between *The Final Friday* and *Jason X*, since the opening of the film sees Jason stuck in hell and Freddy deciding to use him to help him regain power in the waking world. This also takes the sixth *Nightmare* film into account as well, showing Freddy at a low point of power reserves, due to his vanquishing in that one. In terms of picking up where the previous writers had left off, it shows that *Final Friday* is still in play, and the events of the film actually happened, and that somehow, Freddy is able to restore Jason to life on Earth.

There are a few factors that help indicate when *Freddy vs. Jason* is set, and exactly how long our boy was stuck down in the inferno. Late in the film, there's a billboard visible for some property that will be available in the spring of 2004. It's hard to peg down when the film takes place, but school is in session, and the buildings still have a way to go in terms of construction, so the most likely time frame would be the fall of 2003, shortly after the beginning of the school year. That would place it in the same year as *Final Friday*, and Jason had been in hell for a short while before Freddy tracked him down to use him.

Breaking continuity, however, is the general look of the killer, since he's lost the lumpy, long-haired, melted mask look of *Final Friday* and has an entirely new aesthetic, one that's also independent of his appearance in *Jason X*. His skin is smooth again, but now has a bluish tone, and although he's mostly bald again, he does still retain a few random tufts of hair. His outfit has changed once again, ditching the jumpsuit stylings and reverting to a more classic look, adding an oversized jacket for the fall season, ever the fashionable slasher. He's lost the button-down shirt look, opting instead for a gray sweatshirt over a navy blue undershirt. It's a bit of a minor note, but it's the first time in the series that he is not wearing a collared shirt. The mask is given a sort of reboot, and appears to be new acquisition. It's missing any of the previous battle marks, but does still seem to be old and beat up. The origin of this mask is unknown, as he's just wearing it when we first see him in hell. Considering that the mask he wore in *Final Friday* was shown to have remained on Earth after he was sucked underground, it would have been necessary to acquire a new one, and it can be assumed that it was just a part of the hellscape that he donned. As in *Final Friday*, there is no face reveal here, and the closest the audience gets to seeing his kisser is a brief moment near the ending in which the mask is slightly lifted, exposing the lower half of his face. Pictures do exist, and they show a somewhat less zombified form. In fact, the new makeup has a resemblance to the classic look of the killer, but has a more scar-riddled, Frankenstein-esque look.

Since Hodder didn't return to the role, his characteristics have also changed. He's less aggressive here, slower and more methodical than the previous actor's angry, rage-filled demeanor. This is due to the part being taken on by Ken Kirzinger, a stuntman who previously had played a small part in *Jason Takes Manhattan*. Yu's intention was to have Jason be seen as the lesser of the two evils, and he wanted a more sympathetic portrayal to the character. It's theorized that he was chosen over Hodder for size reasons, given that Kirzinger had a few inches on Robert

Jason (Ken Kirzinger) shows off a simpler, classic look (*Freddy Vs. Jason*, New Line, 2003).

Englund and the idea was to have a Jason that literally towered over Freddy. Fans were pretty dismayed by the announcement, with some viewing Hodder as the signature actor for the role.

Possibly the most contentious element the film adds comes later on, as Jason is brought into the dream world to combat Freddy. While there, the dream demon discovers that a wall of water will stop Jason in his tracks, while declaring that it appears to be the one thing that the behemoth fears. Fans of the series take great issue with this, considering that Voorhees has been shown, on multiple occasions, to willingly enter water. He emerges from the lake in Part 4, *The Final Chapter,* to kill a girl in a raft and submerges himself to confront Tommy Jarvis at the end of *Part VI.* There are numerous other instances where he's around water, and he has never shown this fear before. It should be noted, however, that this only occurs in the dream world of Jason's mind. An argument can be made that this is a subconscious fear, one that only exists in the recesses of his thoughts, a deep-down memory of his drowning. Perhaps the trauma of dying, or almost dying (depending on which version of the story is the truth), has stuck with him through his adventures, and although on an outward level, shows no fear when confronted with some good ol' H_2O, he still retains the fear in his lizard brain.

Although it's titled *Freddy vs. Jason,* the film feels more like a *Nightmare on Elm Street* entry than a *Friday the 13th* one, with very little aspects of Crystal Lake and the Voorhees history, save for a local deputy reading off the killer's backstory. The majority of the storyline takes place in Springfield, Krueger territory, but does manage to end up at the infamous campground for the final battle. As mentioned earlier, there's a new set of condos being built beside the lake, because the residents of that town apparently never learn. It's feasible that the area truly believes Jason to be dead now, since his most recent exploits ended up with him being blown into tiny pieces. It can be assumed that the killing that happened afterward, with the possessed people, were probably attributed to copycats, and that that part of the story isn't general knowledge—but even if it were, that ends with Jason being dragged down into hell, so in either scenario, Crystal Lake probably thinks that their Voorhees troubles are over. Of course, they never are.

Since the film was promised as a battle to the death between the two terror titans, and they promised that there would be a clear victor, one of the two had to face defeat. The battle ends with Jason losing several fingers and receiving a large number of wounds before he finally proves to be the winner of the fight, impaling Freddy with his own arm. Before the credits roll, we see him emerge from the depths of the lake, Krueger's head in his hands.

Since *Jason X* told us that he's been in captivity and they attempted to execute him in 2008, this actually leaves him in position for that movie, as at some point during the next five years, he ends up being captured and tried, so in terms of a series continuity, this actually does bridge the gap between those two previous films. Also, presumably, that healing factor they mentioned allowed him to fully regrow the fingers that had been chopped off.

The budget for *Freddy vs. Jason* was a previously unheard number for a film involving Jason: $30 million. This was ten times as much money as most of the previous films, and would cost more than the entire Paramount collection combined. It was as big a risk as they've taken with either character, but with a couple of decades of buildup, they seemed to think it was a safe bet.

The hype was strong for the battle, and a considerable amount of promotion was done, including a boxing-style weigh-in. It all paid off as *Freddy vs. Jason* would take the number 1 spot in its opening weekend, bringing in $36 million. It would remain in the top spot the following weekend, earning a grand total of around $115 million worldwide by the end of its run.[12] It became the highest-grossing entry of the series, and remains so to this day.

Although *FvJ* brought that section of the timeline to a close, the story did almost continue. A planned sequel, entitled *Freddy vs. Jason vs. Ash*, in which the villains would return to battle the protagonist of the *Evil Dead* series, was written and worked its way through various stages of preproduction before being canceled. The script was later adapted into comic book form, showing how the proposed story would have furthered the franchise. It would establish that Freddy was not, in fact, dead at the end of the movie, and would again manipulate Jason to serve his ends. It would incorporate the inclusion of the Necronomicon from *The Final Friday* in order to bring Ash into continuity. A follow-up series actually utilized the abandoned threads of Tommy Jarvis and Neil Gordon, as well as a number of other characters from the franchise, including *Part VII*'s Tina, *Part VIII*'s Remy, and the Kimballs from *Jason Goes to Hell*. It does play a bit of havoc with the series timeline, since the characters' ages are all over the place. Most of the characters do not seem to have aged at all, yet Stephanie Kimball, last seen as an infant, is now in her teens. That would seem to be stating that it takes place at least 15 years after *The Final Friday*, yet Tina and Remy are both still depicted in their early 20s or so. Since neither of these were ever filmed, it's easy to discount both comic series as non-canon—particularly since the time frame of when things are set, and how everything wraps up, does potentially create a snafu regarding the beginnings of *Jason X*.

By this point, remakes of classic horror franchises had started cropping up left and right, so it was only a matter of time before it would be Jason's turn. So, six years after killing his biggest rival, they decided to give it a go with 2009's *Friday the 13th*. This would mark the first time that the actual title had been used in almost 20 years. This was in part due to a unique deal, since this entry produced neither by Paramount, nor by New Line. Instead, Platinum Dunes, Michael Bay's production company, did the honors. Having come off a successful reboot of the *Texas Chainsaw Massacre*, Jason was next on their agenda. They managed to get the rights to the film, including the title, by allowing Paramount to retain the international distribution rights, while New Line did so in the US.

The biggest issue when it comes to doing a remake of a franchise is deciding exactly where to start. The initial concept was to start at the very beginning and do an origin story, showing Jason as a young boy and depicting the events that would eventually lead up to him becoming a killer. It's possible that Platinum Dunes' approach was to make a soft reboot and do a film that could potentially just be the prequel to what had happened before, and have a spot in the existing continuity, or it could start it all over again and be viewed as a new beginning. At one point, there was even a possibility of the incorporation of Tommy Jarvis.

After this idea was scrapped, the screenwriters were left with a different series of issues. If you do a remake of the first film, you're not including Jason, who by this point is the entire selling point of the series. If you decide to do the second film, you're using the bag head version, eliminating the most identifiable element of the character, the hockey mask. If you want your film to include your most recognizable character, in his most recognizable look, you essentially have to go with the third movie. Producer Michael Bay decided to just go ahead and do all three.

We start off with a pre-credit sequence that shows us the finale of the very first film, with Alice killing Pamela Voorhees. It actually gives us a date for this segment, placing her death in 1980, the year the original film was released. Unlike the original, however, this version shows us a young Jason lurking nearby, witnessing the decapitation of his mother, thus solidifying one of the longest-running questions of the regular series. Some of the timeframe is a bit obscured, but it appears in this version of events that Pamela's rampage occurred immediately after the seeming drowning death of Jason. He had, however, somehow survived the drowning, only to then see his mom get killed, driving him off the deep end.

The bulk of the movie takes place in what it calls present day, but they actually have a few contradictions to that. One of the characters claims the camp was closed down 20 years ago, which would seem to imply that it's actually around the year 2000 or so, but later in the film there's a license plate that expires in 2008. It could easily be a slight production issue, and not meant to be seen, but the plate is front and center in the frame, a detail that the crew would surely be aware of. Seeing a concrete date printed out seems a more plausible clue to the time frame than another character's ghost story version of the legend, so it's the more likely answer. It's more likely that the setting is 2008, and the character's story is wrong, and that he meant to state that it was about 30 years ago instead.

When we first meet this interpretation of our killer, he's more in line with the second film's look, sporting the bag over his head. He's been returned to his default settings, free of all the damage of the last 11 films, and is fully human once again. No longer the slow, lumbering zombie, we're once again given a full-speed, running Jason, chasing his victims at a frightening pace. One other wrinkle we're introduced to, one that's unique to this incarnation, is that Jason sets traps for his victims, showing a level of intelligence that we haven't really seen from the character before. Along with that is the notion that he's built a series of underground tunnels in which he lives and travels, accounting for his ability to randomly appear in different parts of the camp. With this, it's likely that this Jason can't teleport, assuming that was an ability of the original one in the first place.

We also see this Jason do something else that we haven't seen before: take a hostage. A young victim, who happens to look like his mother, is kept in the tunnels with no real harm being done to her. This is often criticized as being an odd deviation for the character, since

Remake Jason (Derek Mears): back to basics (*Friday the 13th*, Warner Bros./New Line, 2009).

we've only ever seen him interested in killing trespassers, but it's easy to note that this is not the incarnation that we are familiar with, and is a completely new identity. Therefore, any new traits or quirks are just facets of this new version, and remain in character.

About halfway through the film, Jason's sack is pulled off of his head, and instead of just putting it back on, he chooses a nearby replacement, donning the trademark hockey mask and becoming the villain that we were expecting. His face is never really revealed, although glimpses of it are shown, and a quick pause-button finger allows a good view of it. He's not dissimilar to the look of the early film, probably being closest to the design of the third film, but with the hair tufts of the second. His clothing remains fairly consistent, looking vaguely similar to his stylings from *Freddy vs. Jason*, with the most notable alteration being the ditching of both the collared shirt and the sweatshirt, running with a simple T-shirt look.

In the climatic final fight, he's dispatched fairly easily, with a strangulation by chain and a machete to the heart, although a last-minute jump scare indicates that he's still alive, giving a callback to the first film's "jumping from the lake" stinger.

While not quite the budget given to *Freddy vs. Jason*, it still had a healthy price tag of $19 million, which was comparable to the other Platinum Dunes horror remakes. Its performance at the box office was a mixed bag. Its opening weekend looked very promising, as it collected just over $45 million, taking the number 1 spot. It would overtake *FvJ* as having the biggest opening weekend for the series. In fact, on its first day of release, it pulled in $19 million, which was more than the entire runs of *Parts 7, 8, 9* and *10*. However, in its second weekend, it would fall off massively, dropping off around 80 percent in ticket sales, and would finish its run at around $92 million worldwide.[13] So, although this number would easily exceed the grosses of almost every other entry, it would fall short of beating its immediate predecessor's tally, and remains the second highest-grossing film in the franchise.

Even though a sequel was planned, it never happened, although information seems to imply that it would have taken place during the winter, and show Jason in the snow, something had not been seen in the films. It was to be titled *Friday the 13th: Camp Blood—The Death of Jason Voorhees*, and would once again promise to end the franchise for good, although Rocky the Squirrel would most likely remind us: "that trick never works." A handful of script pages have been released online, revealing that Whitney, the 2009 film's Final Girl, had indeed been killed. This version never happened, since New Line relinquished their rights, leaving Paramount to go it alone.

Instead of moving forward with a sequel to that film, the plans were to reboot the series once again, although production was canceled for a rather unusual reason. The movie *Rings*, the third part of the American version of the *Ringu* series, bombed at the box office, convincing the studio that horror films were not a profitable avenue to take at that time, so they shelved the script. It was a really unusual move, considering the film was mere weeks away from when it was to begin shooting, but again, some information about it has made it into the hands of the general public. Similar to the 2009 version, they were once again faced with how to restart the story, and which aspect to focus on. And once again, they seemed to just go with all of them. It was to take place in 1977, at Camp Crystal Lake, and feature Jason as a child while there's a number of mysterious murders going on. It would be revealed that this was the handiwork of Elias Voorhees, Jason's father, and he would be stopped by Pamela. Apparently, this portion would encompass the first third of the film, and ended with the boy's presumed drowning. Then it would transition to 1980, and the next third would follow Pamela, stricken with grief, commencing her own rampage, and would end with her being killed, much like the first film. Finally, the last act would jump ahead again, to a 19-year-old Jason, now sporting a yellow version of the classic hockey mask, doing his own group of killings. It's unclear how fans would have reacted to this sort of mash-up of the first couple of films, and how disjointed it would feel, switching its killers every half hour or so, although some preproduction stills made their way to the internet. They depict a Jason that looks pretty similar to the classic look, and most resembles the appearance of the fourth film, featuring a weathered, cracked hockey mask.

The series has been in limbo ever since, with a lawsuit holding up any plans for any additional entries, although a resolution was reached in late 2021. The lawsuit placed certain rights directly in the hands of Victor Miller, giving him sole claim to the original screenplay and characters within. As a result, Paramount and Sean S. Cunningham are unable to use the character of Jason Voorhees without express permission from Miller. However, since the adult, hockey-mask-wearing version of the killer doesn't appear in the first film, Miller does not have the rights to that. Therefore, Cunningham theoretically could make a movie about a hulking, goalie-inspired slasher at a campground; he just can't call that killer Jason Voorhees, nor the campground Crystal Lake. Time will tell if any sort of agreement can be reached between the two entities involved, because until then, the franchise will stay in limbo. Worth mentioning is the fact that Miller's lawyer in the case was Larry Zerner, notable for portraying the character of Shelly in the third film. There's a small irony in the fact that the actor that is most known for playing the guy who helped shape our image of the character of Jason has become partly responsible for helping to make sure that character remains absent from the screen.

Outside of the films, and not a part of the official canon and time-line, there exists a healthy amount of other media featuring Jason. Along with a collection of novels adapting the films, there were also several young adult tales released in the '90s that featured different characters finding Jason's mask and being possessed by his evil. As such, the killer himself did not actually appear in these books, and if one so desired, they could be considered a part of the regular series. In the early 2000s, there were also two sets of novels put out by a company called Black Flame. One of these series followed the events of *Jason X* and led to four books of adventures, with Uber-Jason landing on Earth 2 to continue his escapades. Because this time frame has never actually been covered in the films, it's easily accepted that these could be considered canon follow-ups to the 10th film, representing the actual further fate of the character. The other line of books would pick up after *FvJ* and is looser with continuity, merely detailing what happens to Jason after his face-off with Krueger. Since the timing of these would possibly contradict Mr. Voorhees ending up in the custody of the military, they are most likely thought of as their own separate continuity.

As mentioned earlier, there are also several different versions of *Friday the 13th* comics, going all the way back to the '90s. Topps Comics released an adaptation of the ninth film, and then branched into an original tale, having Jason face off against Leatherface. Later, in the mid–2000s, Avatar Comics would pick up the rights, releasing their own take on the character, picking up after the events of *Freddy vs. Jason*. Like the Black Flame novels, these would most likely not be considered canon with the films, since they would end with Voorhees in a place contradictory to the events of *Jason X*. Speaking of that film, Avatar would also put out a comic continuation of it, actually having a fight between the Uber-Jason version and the standard version, which again could possibly considered as the actual follow-up to *Jason X*. Shortly afterward, Wildstorm, a division of DC Comics, would take a crack at it, releasing several miniseries that don't really occur at any particular point of the continuity, which can be viewed as completely separate from the film universe. They did, however, put out a couple of prequels, delving into the series' past. One focused on Pamela, detailing her life before the first film, and another explored the past of Crystal

Lake itself and the evil that took place to give it the reputation of being "cursed."

There have also been several video games to feature the franchise, with the first coming out all the way back in 1986. Later adaptations came for the NES and mobile phones, but the most notorious wouldn't arrive until 2017 with *Friday the 13th: The Game*. It would be a multiplayer experience in which you were able to choose between being a camp counselor or Jason himself, and also featured some story elements with details from the films. It would allow you to choose from any of the killer's incarnations from the various films, including Roy, as well as including film characters such as Tommy Jarvis, *Part III's* Shelly, and biker girl Fox from *Part III* as well. However, due to the same legal wrangles that plagued the film, the game would also be shut down, and while it's still available to play, the official servers have also been shut down.

It would also be remiss to not mention the television show, *Friday the 13th: The Series*, which ran for 72 episodes, from 1987 to 1990. It was developed by Frank Mancuso, Jr., although under the title of *The 13th Hour*. When it was decided that it might dissuade new viewers, they took on the *Friday* name in order to appear to a larger audience. Despite the name, the show would actually have nothing to do with the films, and featured none of the characters. Instead, it would focus on an antique store full of cursed objects. Each week, the store's owners would have to find one of the objects, which would give their holders a unique ability that would come with a deadly price. The idea was floated at one point to introduce the notion that Jason's mask was one of the cursed objects, but that was abandoned to let the show stand on its own. Even though the premise caused confusion among viewers expecting to see a show about a camp slasher, it would actually be very successful at its onset. It became popular enough to move the show's time slot from a late-night position to prime time. Although it did quite well, the decision was made partway through the third season to cancel the show. The announcement was extremely abrupt, the crew was not given enough time to deal with the information, and there was no chance to film any sort of conclusion to the show. Because of that, there is no finality to the series, and the final episode is just a typical one, detailing the recovery of another cursed item. Interestingly, John D. Lemay, one of the leads of the show, would go on to become one of the main characters of *Jason Goes to Hell*, although he would be playing a completely different character, keeping the entities separate.

There have also been several other attempts to bring the franchise to the small screen in a more official capacity. Back in the early 2000s,

Cunningham spoke about the possibility of a show called the *Crystal Lake Chronicles*, which would focus more on the teenagers inhabiting the town, comparing it to shows like *Buffy the Vampire Slayer*. According to Cunningham, Jason would not be a main character of the show, and instead would act more as a recurring background element. Another attempt occurred around 2014, with the intention of doing a series for the CW, simply entitled *Friday the 13th*. This one would be truer to the spirit of the films, focusing on a detective at Crystal Lake, looking for his missing brother and dealing with a returned Jason Voorhees, as well as discovering new details about his family's past. This version made it to script level, and some development was done, but it never made it to the production stage, as CW president Mark Pedowitz stated that he just couldn't envision the series going beyond the pilot episode.

At this point, it remains extremely unclear if we will ever see the series return, and in which incarnation it might do so. It's currently been close to 15 years without seeing the killer on film, marking the longest gap without an entry in the series' history. It appears clear, however, that when we next see it, it will undoubtably once again depict a fresh start for the characters.

Timeline Summary

Friday the 13th—June 1979 (date given on the tombstone in *The Final Chapter*)

Friday the 13th Part 2—Early summer 1984 (five-year gap noted by Paul at the campfire)

Friday the 13th Part III—Early summer 1984 (news report places it right after the end of *Part 2*)

Friday the 13th: The Final Chapter—Early summer 1984 (picks up immediately after *Part III*)

Friday the 13th: A New Beginning—October 1989 (five years based on Tommy's age difference between films)

Friday the 13th Part VI: Jason Lives—Early summer 1990 (seemingly a short time after *A New Beginning*, but also set at the beginning of a summer season)

Friday the 13th Part VII: The New Blood—May 2000 (10-year gap given for Tina's aging, time confirmed by the film's director)

Friday the 13th Part VIII: Jason Takes Manhattan—Early summer 2002 (enough time given for Jason's rampage to not be recent, and taking place past school graduation)

Jason Goes to Hell: The Final Friday—Early summer 2003 (enough time given for Jason to return to Crystal Lake and military to mount offensive)

Freddy vs. Jason—Fall 2003 (based upon the condo development signs)

Jason X—2010/2465 (based on dialogue given from characters within)

Remake Timeline

Friday the 13th (2009)—1980/2008 (earlier time is shown on-screen, later date is given on a license plate registration sticker)

CHAPTER 2

Halloween

Although the first is considered one of the most well-made horror films of all time, the remainder of the *Halloween* series isn't as highly regarded. In terms of film continuity, the franchise is a double-edged sword. On one hand, it handles its timeline surprisingly well, with only moderate burps in consistency. On the other hand, it's never clear what actually counts, since the series restarts itself on a regular basis.

The debut film arrived back in 1978, directed by John Carpenter; it was one of his earliest feature films. He had just come off *Assault on Precinct 13*, and producers Irwin Yablans and Moustapha Akkad approached him about this little idea of theirs: a killer that stalks babysitters. Carpenter went to work on the script, along with his collaborator and then-girlfriend, Debra Hill. Yablans had wanted to make a film that had the impact of *The Exorcist*, and it's clear that a certain amount of inspiration was also drawn from the earlier *Black Christmas*, but much of the Celtic inspirations of the storyline were straight from Carpenter and Hill. The first draft didn't include these elements and was crafted under the title *The Babysitter Murders*, but Yablans was the one who suggested the Halloween setting, which the writers then ran with.

It kicks off in 1963, which it's nice enough to tell us with a big graphic up on the screen. We witness an unseen killer attacking and murdering a teenage girl, only to have the perpetrator revealed to be the girl's younger brother, Michael Myers. He's six years old at the time, and still wearing a clown costume from trick-or-treating. We then jump ahead 15 years to Halloween night in 1978, the same year the film was released. We're introduced to psychiatrist Sam Loomis, played by veteran actor Donald Pleasence. The role was actually written for Peter Cushing, who had just finished a big role in *Star Wars*, but he balked at the low salary offer. Christopher Lee was also offered the role, although he passed as well, a decision he later admitted to regretting. When Michael escapes custody and goes home, he begins stalking random teenage girls, and I think it's important to stress the word *random*. At the time of filming, there was no consideration of any family links that would appear in later films, and the idea was that Michael just chose these girls because they were there. One of those girls is played by a young Jamie Lee Curtis in the role that made her famous, Laurie Strode. Originally, Carpenter was hesitant to cast her, as he had other actresses in mind, but realized that Curtis's family connections (her parents were megastars Tony Curtis and Janet Leigh) would serve as good publicity for the film.

Michael's appearance is definitely a more stable look than that of Jason Voorhees, although, as you'll see, had its own fluctuations. All of his hallmarks are established in this film, however, with the iconic white face mask and blue coveralls, which would remain throughout the series. As noted time and time again, the mask is a repainted William Shatner face, hair teased out into tufts. Oddly, even though it's pretty hard to just look at it and think of it as being the image of Captain Kirk, when viewed with its original paint scheme, it's painfully, obviously Shatner. The mask was used due to budget, as Tommy Lee Wallace, the film's production designer, just went to a local costume shop and bought the cheapest mask he could find. He came across the Shatner mask for $1.98, purchased it, then took it back to widen the eye holes and paint it. The blue coveralls come from a mechanic that Michael kills after escaping the institution, coincidentally the same size as him.

There is a pretty strong establishment of the characters here, which will fluctuate as the series progresses, but we are given their initial starting points. Loomis is depicted as a very headstrong, but impulsive man, somewhat obsessed with the concept of Michael as a vessel of ultimate evil. At times, he seems to be as crazed as Michael himself, but he

Michael Myers (Nick Castle) by the iconic hedge (*Halloween*, Compass International, 1978).

has a more altruistic motive. When we first meet Laurie, she is shown to be a somewhat naive, fairly chaste young woman with a very tenacious streak. It would be easy to dismiss her character as a standard Final Girl archetype, but it must be taken into account that she was one of the original templates for the trope. It could be argued that she helped to really define the role, since her predecessors, such as Sally from *The Texas Chainsaw Massacre* and Jess from *Black Christmas*, took more evasive tactics with their attackers. Laurie, however, would show more of a willingness to fight back against her foe.

From a story standpoint, it's a pretty simple tale. Michael encounters three girls on the street and decides to follow them around, eventually killing them, one by one, until only Laurie remains. There's no real backstory to Michael and the reasoning for his madness, which is part of what makes the character so terrifying. As opposed to the trope of a villain being abused or living a tortured life, essentially creating the monster that they would become, it's instead implied that Michael's evil is innate. It didn't matter what his upbringing was. He was just born evil. It is established that he's rather absurdly strong, although his strength is on a human level, and he seems to be extremely resistant to damage and pain. There is really nothing supernatural attributed to this, but there is a suggestion of a greater evil being present, with subtle ideas of an evil force guiding Michael. Although, to counteract this, near the ending, Laurie is temporarily able to unmask Michael. Whereas the entire film had propped him up to be this form of ultimate evil, giving him untold menace, we see his face for one brief moment, and he appears to merely be a man. During the climax of the film, he's stabbed in the eye with a coat hanger, has a knife stuck in him, and is shot by Loomis six times. Six times. After all this, he's still able to get back up again, vanishing in the last shots of the film, leaving it open for some sort of continuation. I mean, the ending all but flashes "to be continued..." up on the screen.

It's important to note that Carpenter had not really considered the option of doing a sequel, even if the ending was perfectly tailored to one. He just wanted the ending to be ambiguous, leaving the audience guessing about who Michael was and what he was capable of doing.

The film was shot on a tiny budget of around $300,000, which would translate to about $1.3 million today. This was considered a fairly low-budget film at the time, especially compared to heavy hitters like *The Exorcist*, which had a budget of $12 million in 1972 money. Even *Black Christmas*, the film it draws the most comparison to, cost around double *Halloween*'s budget. But the slasher was a huge hit, grossing $47 million in the US and drawing another $23 million in international box office, giving it a grand total of around $70 million worldwide,[1] an achievement that earned it a spot as one of the most successful independent films of all time.

Surprisingly, or I guess not so surprisingly if you're familiar with the treatment of horror films, it was lambasted by critics. Although many praised its atmosphere and general moodiness, others called it unoriginal and derivative of Hitchcock. One critic who did not tear it apart was Roger Ebert. Considering how he viewed the *Friday the 13th* films, this seems unusual, but the Chicago reviewer actually named it as one his top 10 films of that year.

One thing was for sure, though: with that level of success, Michael Myers was bound to return.

Against the better judgement of John Carpenter, he did. The original film's director really didn't want to return to the series, preferring instead to move on to new projects, but did stick around to produce a sequel as well as handling the writing duties. Directorial duties were instead handed off to Rick Rosenthal, his debut in that role, and three years later, in 1981, *Halloween II* arrived.

At the time, Carpenter was pretty preoccupied with trying to get *The Fog* off the ground, and viewed the task of writing the sequel as more of a chore than anything. His initial draft of the screenplay actually jumped ahead several years, with Michael tracking Laurie down to an apartment building and antagonizing her once more. This was altered as revisions went on, with the setting changing to that of a hospital, and the time gap being reduced dramatically. There were a few advantages evident in the writing process. The first was that it was Carpenter and Hill picking up from their own script, so there could be a certain consistency to the narrative. The second was that the finale of the first film was so open-ended that finding a place to pick up from was no trouble at all. With bridging the gap between the two entries being a non-issue, that just left shaping a new story to tell.

With the exception of John Carpenter behind the camera, almost everyone who was in front of it returned for the second entry. Jamie Lee Curtis reprised her role as Laurie, Donald Pleasence returned as Loomis; Charles Cypher returned in the smaller role of Leigh Brackett. Nancy Stephens, who had a minor role in the first film as nurse Marion Chambers, returned as well, in a larger role. One actor who didn't return was Nick Castle, who played Michael. He had decided to leave acting and stunt work behind and try his hand at directing, going on to helm *Tag: The Assassination Game*, *The Last Starfighter*, *The Boy Who Could Fly*, and several others. Instead, the part was filled by Dick Warlock, who had been an established stunt man in the industry.

The film actually picks up immediately after the events of the first one, taking place all in the same night. The entire bulk of the action of both films occurs over a very short amount of time, with the second one mostly taking place in the wee hours of the morning after Halloween night, so most likely November 1, 1978. The direct flow of the two movies creates the feeling of watching one continual story, instead of being one being a sequel to the other.

An interesting aspect of continuity is the appearance of Ben Tramer, a character briefly mentioned in the first film, who is seen here for the first time. After Loomis mistakes a trick-or-treater for Michael, he pulls his gun, causing the teen to run away and get hit by car. Later, that corpse is revealed to be that of Tramer, and it should be noted that we never see him without the mask, so over the course of two movies, the character is never actually seen. Also interesting is the fact that Loomis, who is not a police officer, suffers no consequence for being the catalyst of the chain of events. He pulls a gun out in the middle of a crowded intersection with dozens of innocent civilians nearby, causing one of them to run into the street and get hit by a car, and the police pretty much just shrug.

The biggest and most important aspect of the storyline that this film brings into play is the notion that Laurie is Michael's sister, revealing a motivation for his obsession that was absent from the first film. It's revealed that after her parents died, she was put up for adoption and raised by the Strode family. Given that Laurie is 17 during the first film, and that Michael would be 21 during that same time frame, there's four years between them. Since Michael was six years old when he killed his older sister, that would mean that a two-year-old Laurie was somewhere in that house when the murder was occurring, and that his sisterly bloodlust didn't extend to babies. This plot point was introduced in order to give a rationale for Michael to continue hunting the young girl, a decision that he later referred to as silly, although it would go to be a driving focus of the later entries. It's important to note that the concept of Laurie as Michael's sister was not a part of the first film, and was never intended to be. This concept was only born during the writing process of the second film.

One minor alteration in the continuity between the films is the look of Michael himself. The shape and appearance of the mask changes, as does the look of the hair. Strangely enough, the mask is the same between the two films, and the inconsistencies were not intended. The change from Castle to Warlock accounted for the change of the mask shape, as Dick's head was wider, filling it out more and making it look like a tighter fit overall. Also, in the years between filming, the hair became matted and gnarled, causing them to push it back more,

Part 2's wide face Michael (as portrayed by Dick Warlock) (*Halloween II*, Universal, 1981).

exposing the forehead area further. The coloration of the mask also changed with age, taking on a slight yellowish tinge. His outfit remains the same, as he wears the same coveralls from the first film.

One of the biggest differences between the sequel and the first film were in the increased levels of nudity and gore. Whereas most of the original's violence occurred off-screen or was carried out more subtly, in this film you'll get a shot of a syringe entering a person's eyeball. This decision actually came from Carpenter himself, who realized the changing atmosphere of the horror industry. In the time after the release of *Halloween*, a number of imitators would arise, each one upping the violence and breast quotient. It was decided that if *Halloween II* was going to measure up, they would have to match that increase in intensity. His decision was so firm that he would end up stepping in near the end of filming to reshoot several of the kills to make them more violent. Rosenthal has stated that he was unhappy with the additions that were made, and that they damaged the films pacing. One thing that's for sure is that it does represent a jarring change in tone between the two films.

In terms of character consistency, there were definitely some minor alterations made. Loomis has suddenly become more frantic, more erratic, in his behavior. He has become more impulsive and prone to waving his gun around, causing the aforementioned death of Ben Tramer, and at one point shooting out the window of a car that he is riding in to make a point. Laurie, on the other hand, is fairly consistent, although she is sidelined for the bulk of the film. She spends the majority of the runtime unconscious in a hospital bed, only becoming fully aware of what's going on in the final reel. Until Michael arrives at the hospital and commits several murders, she is essentially a non-character, with the story focusing on several side characters instead.

One of those side characters would be Jimmy, played by Lance Guest, who is treated as the possible male lead of the film. He's tied to the storyline in that his younger brother goes to school with Laurie, and he appears to be smitten with her. He becomes a somewhat important character in the series mythology, but in the film itself, his fate is uncertain. During the course of Michael's rampage, Jimmy discovers the body of one of his victims. He manages to slip and fall on the pool of blood, hitting his head on the ground. Later, he's seen in a car, but he passes out behind the wheel. He's not seen again after this, so it's unclear whether or not this was intended to represent the death of his character, but in the television version of the film, things go a little differently. In this version, as Laurie is taken away in an ambulance, Jimmy is also there, bandages wrapped around his noggin. He and Laurie embrace, happy to see each other alive, confirming his survival—but only if you consider this alternate version to be canon. It has been theorized that the two would end up becoming involved romantically, and Jimmy would father one of Laurie's children who would be seen in later installments, but nothing has ever been confirmed.

There is also an expansion of the theme of Halloween being a cursed night that was established in the first film, and a general darkness that has encompassed the town. There are small riots, a boy who had bitten into razor blade–laden candy, and the talk of Samhain as a night of evil. It's effective and slightly enhances the very subtle tones of supernatural influence, without making it an overt plot point.

The film's finale creates quite the issue for future installments, since the intention was to give closure to the storyline. Considering that Carpenter wasn't really interested in sequels in general, he chose to end the film with a definitive death for Michael Myers. He figured that if he killed the villain in a method that couldn't be easily explained away, the producers would have no choice but to end the storyline. So, after stalking and killing the staff of the hospital that Laurie was recuperating in, the final confrontation sees Laurie, Michael, and Loomis squaring off. This ends with the teenage girl managing to shoot the killer's eyes out, blinding him. There is a minor issue with his one eye working in the first place, due to Laurie's well-placed hanger to the iris in the first film, but it can be easily theorized that the damage was minor and didn't hamper his vision. This is followed by Loomis igniting the room full of gas to explode and burn, with Laurie narrowly escaping. With the doctor in the room when it goes up, and Myers seen stumbling out, fully engulfed in flames and last seen burning away, it would seem to be the end of the obsessed brother's rampage.

The sequel came with an enhanced price tag of $2.5 million, almost ten times the cost of the original, and although it did not quite reach the heights of that one, it was still considered a financial success. On its opening weekend, it pulled it close to $7.5 million, already making back its budget and then some. Over the course of its run, it would go on to accumulate a total of $25 million,[2] becoming the second highest-grossing horror film of the year, only losing out to *An American Werewolf in London*. It was denied some of the box office potential of the original due to being banned in a portion of Europe.

Critically, it fared about as well as its forerunner, with most denouncing it as standard horror fare. Even Ebert referred to it as a massive step down from the original, noting that it had more in common with the *Halloween* imitators than the film itself. It did receive its fair share of accolades, even if they were mostly halfhearted and referred to the film as being better than some of the more exploitative examples of the genre.

But then things got weird. It seems that the producers still wanted more *Halloween* movies, because it was clearly a lucrative product, but with the storyline ended, how would they continue? Well, Carpenter's idea was simple. His idea was to treat the *Halloween* series as an anthology, with a movie released every year, the only thematic link being that they would all center around the holiday. In fact, Carpenter and Hill would only agree to contribute to the third entry if it were *not* a continuation of the previous two films, and instead created a completely new and original concept.

Because of this, in 1982, *Halloween III: Season of the Witch* was unleashed into the world. Carpenter remained in the producer role, but again chose to not direct, and also passed on the writing job, even though he is said to have some say in the overall story. Instead, Tommy Lee Wallace came aboard, in his directorial debut, while also doing scripting duties. Wallace had been a childhood friend of Carpenter's, and worked with him on several of his previous films, including the first *Halloween*. He had the distinction of actually being Michael Myers at one point, playing the character during parts of the iconic closet attack scene. Wallace had been previously offered the second film, although he declined due to dissatisfaction with the script. When the opportunity arose again, with the chance to also write the film, he jumped at the chance.

Of course, the film is once again set around Halloween. Conveniently, a screen graphic tells us that it begins on Friday, October 23 and spans all the way until October 31, which it tells us is a Sunday. Those days and dates actually line up with the year 1982, giving us a timeframe for the film. This does assume that those dates would coincide with how they landed in our world, but unless something contradicts that, there doesn't appear to be any reason to believe otherwise.

The story goes in a much different direction than the previous films, obviously, having to basically start fresh with the concept. What we get instead of a murderous Michael Myers is a mystery plot involving killer Halloween masks, robot assassins, and Stonehenge. Yes, you read that right. The primary villain of the film turns out to be one of the giant rocks from Stonehenge. It's a choice.

Tom Atkins was brought in to be the leading man, having previously been in Carpenter's *The Fog* and *Escape from New York*. Most of his other work was television roles and smaller movie parts, so working in horror films allowed him the chance to play the lead. *RoboCop*'s Old Man himself, Dan O'Herlihy, stepped into the villain role, giving the film an air of respectability. Most of the other parts were filled with bit part and character actors, although Dick Warlock would return briefly to play an android killer. Jamie Lee Curtis also returned in a very limited capacity, serving as the voice-over for the town's curfew system, as well as a phone operator.

In terms of continuity, since it's not really connected to the previous two films, there's no consistency at all. Every character is new, as are the situations and settings. Instead of taking place in Haddonfield, Illinois, we move to the fictional town of Santa Mira, California, the same setting for the original *Invasion of the Body Snatchers*. This was actually a sort of hint to the film's nature, since it's not so much about a man hunting you down with a knife, as much as it's a film about being

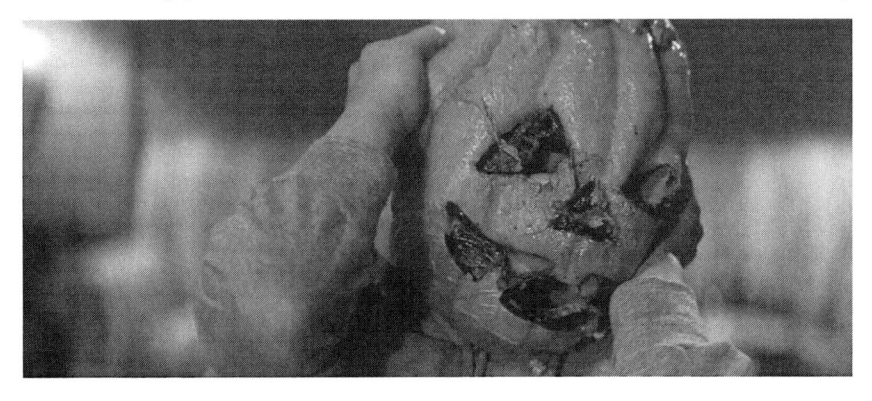

Silver Shamrock's (Brad Schacter) plan in effect (*Halloween III*, Universal, 1982).

replaced. Here, instead of being turned into a pod person, humans are swapped out with robot duplicates.

The film goes out of its way to establish that not only is this a different storyline, it's actually a completely different universe, since at one point, Dr. Challis is locked in a room with a television that's airing the original *Halloween* film, with Jamie Lee Curtis on the screen. Clearly, that establishes that this film is in a separate continuity with its own timeline, as well as providing a nice callback to the soundtrack of the original. As the movie plays, a key part of the first film's score hits, blending with the action on-screen, effectively becoming the score of this movie as well. It's a clever, meta gag that works really well. Some have theorized that this doesn't necessarily confirm that they are in different universes, as the images on the TV could merely be from some sort of reenactment or factionalized version of the actual events that happened in this universe, but it seems more likely that they're just two distinct worlds.

For a long time, *Season of the Witch* was seen as the black sheep of the series, and it remains one of the most lackluster entries as far as box office goes. It only grossed $14 million, which was a pretty dramatic drop from either of the two previous films.[3] Granted, the budget was still a very modest $2.5 million, so it would still amount to a healthy profit for the studio. Still, even though it could still be considered successful, the declining ticket sales scared Yablans and Akkad enough that they pumped the brakes on future plans for the anthology concept.

Fan reaction was extremely negative, as most filmgoers were expecting to see Michael Myers and were very disappointed with his absence. However, time has changed people's perspectives and it's now looked back on as a fun '80s horror film. Many people concede that if it had been released under another name and didn't carry the *Halloween* brand title, it would've been better accepted and might be looked back on more fondly. There are still other fans, myself included, who truly enjoy the film, and would've actually preferred if the series had gone the route that Carpenter wanted, becoming an anthology series telling different tales instead repeating the Myers slasher story repeatedly. But let's face it: when it comes to horror franchises, people tend to like seeing the same story repeated.

So that's what they got. It took a little while, but eventually, producer Moustapha Akkad decided to bring back the franchise. After the theatrical disappointment that was *Halloween III*, he realized that it was important to bring back Michael Myers as the central villain. It was a similar situation to what Paramount found themselves in after the fifth *Friday* film. There was the realization that the Shatner masked murderer was the essential component of the series. John Carpenter was asked to come on board the project, which he considered for a while, working with writer Dennis Etchison on a new script that brought the Shape back. In his version, the first film's kids, Tommy Doyle and Lindsay Wallace, are teenagers now, and they have to face a ghostly Michael Myers powered by the town's own fears. It was a heavier concept that Carpenter loved and Akkad hated, so the original director's interests were bought out and the project moved on without him.

Whoever they brought on board would have a heavy task ahead of them. Like *Friday the 13th Part V,* they were faced with the challenge of continuing a story with a character who had quite clearly been killed off. They brought Alan B. McElroy on board to handle the scripting duties and he pitched the version that made it to the screen. The final version pretty closely resembled his initial concept.

Instead of a ghost Michael, 1988 instead got a more solid version of the slasher, with *Halloween 4: The Return of Michael Myers,* which brought the series back to its roots. It begins with revealing that both Michael and Loomis are still alive, and both managed to survive their wounds from that night. It takes the very simple tactic of saying "Oh, hey. We know that it really looked like these characters died in the last one, but it only looked that way. They're fine." However, Michael is badly burned and in a coma, and for some reason, his face and hands are still covered in bandages. I'm not terribly sure why this would be, since any burn wounds that he would've received would have healed over a very long time ago, so it would just be scar tissue. There really is no reason for them to still have bandages on him, outside of a desire to not show his face on camera. Loomis got off a lot easier, with only minor burns on one side of his face, although I guess he didn't need bandages for his wounds. It's never really explained how either one survived the explosion, although the original script gave a modest reason for it. It featured a scene in which the finale is shown again, and we see that the force of the explosion knocked the good doctor out into a nearby corridor, out of the line of fire of most of the danger, accounting for the moderate scarring he received. As for how Michael survived, not much additional information is given, except for the conceit that he's extremely resistant to damage, which was extremely lucrative for the franchise.

We're told that it's been ten years since his initial rampage, and of course it's Halloween, so that would place this one in October of 1988, putting the series in real time. Michael has been in a vegetative state ever since that night, but is awakened when one of his doctors happens to mention that Laurie has a daughter, and our guy once again has family to kill. It's kind of unclear as to why this particular news would trigger him. He was aware of the fact that his sister was still out there, although it's revealed that she has died in the interim. It's not revealed whether or not he was aware of this fact or not, but it seems as if her death was relatively recent. So, Michael remained in the coma for the entire time in between the hospital incident and her death, knowing that she was still out there, and he remained undisturbed. It can be assumed that he's at some sort of peace, now that she is dead, but that would require some sort of psychic link to her, a supernatural element not yet embraced by the series.

By this time, Jamie Lee Curtis had gone on to a series of pretty successful roles in bigger films and wasn't too excited about returning to the series. There are two opposing stories of whether she was asked or not. Some say that she was asked to reprise the character, but quickly declined. Other accounts state that the producers assumed that due to her recent path of success that she would not be interested, and decided to tailor a new script around her a sense. Either way, without recasting, it became clear that Laurie Strode would not be returning for the newest entry. So instead, the character would have to live on through her family. It is revealed that Laurie and her husband were both killed in an unfortunate car accident. Laurie's daughter, appropriately named Jamie, is this entry's biggest addition to the franchise, becoming the impetus for Michael's obsessions, as he had a void to fill with Curtis not returning. Jamie is either seven or eight years old in the movie, so she would have been born just a few years after the finale of the second film, with many fans theorizing that her father was Jimmy, a minor character from that one, although there is really nothing to substantiate that. There is a brief shot of a photograph of the father, and it does not appear to be Jimmy, or at least Lance Guest. It's possible that it was supposed to be the character recast, although again, there's little to back that up. We learn that the accident has occurred somewhat recently, leaving Jamie to be taken care of family friends. Of course, Michael knows about her now, and comes to kill her.

In terms of Myers's overall appearance, it's mostly consistent with his previous looks, although with slight alterations. For a portion of the film, he remains in the facial bandages. Shortly after getting loose, he attacks a mechanic, gaining a jumpsuit very similar to his previous one, and takes a new mask from a costume shop. This new mask is the same basic concept, but shaped differently. It's rounded out more, with a less menacing facial expression. With wider eyes and less arched eyebrows, he looks a little more confused or shocked than angry. His hair is also a little different, in that it appears to be a bit longer, and mostly pulled back. It was considered to use the mask from the original two films,

Michael's (George P. Wilbur) slicked-back look (*Halloween 4: The Return of Michael Myers*, Trancas International, 1988).

but after those completed filming, and it appeared as if the character were laid to rest, the original prop was given to actor Dick Warlock. The new version seems to have fans split. Some like its blanker look, claiming that it looks more menacing, while others feel it has too much of a clownish appearance.

One of the weirdest aspects of the mask is the single shot in which it completely changes color. Near the end of the film, as Loomis and Jamie are hiding from Michael in a schoolhouse, for a brief moment, it appears as if the famous mask has blondish hair and an almost pink skin tone. The story of the mask is a little confusing, since apparently Don Post Studios, the company hired to create the masks for this movie, accidentally sent over a set of them with the color scheme described above. The makeup crew of the movie were able to actually paint over the masks in order to give the proper color tones, accounting for the extremely pale white, but somehow the incorrect one was used for this one scene. Director Dwight Little has stated that the error was due to a tired crew member rushing in with the incorrect prop. Unfortunately, that means the costuming team didn't notice, the actor wearing it didn't either, the other actors in the scene didn't mention it, and an entire crew including the director, lighting team, sound crew, and all didn't point it out. The other story given is that this is actually a version of the original William Shatner mask, without the painting over that they had done for the originals, so the skin tone and hair color would actually represent the original color scheme of the mask. It seems that the producers wanted to test it out as-is, and shot the school sequence. After viewing

Blondes have more fun, I guess (Donald Pleasance, left, and George P. Wilbur) (*Halloween 4: The Return of Michael Myers*, Trancas International, 1988).

the dailies, they decided they did not like the look at all and decided to reshoot it, with a brand-new mask construction. Although the scene was reshot, the one single instance of the blonde mask managed to make its way into the film.

In a minor note to continuity, since the film takes place on Halloween, Jamie dresses up to go out trick-or-treating and is wearing a clown costume, extremely similar to the one that a young Michael wore on the night that he murdered his sister. It's a minor callback that forms a thematic link in the finale.

Over the course of the film, Michael returns to Haddonfield on Halloween night, stalking and killing a variety of random teens in his search, leading to a face-off in a massive house that for some reason everyone is locked into, even though there are multiple doors and windows shown. After wiping almost everyone out, only Jamie and her adoptive sister remain, and in a final confrontation, police show up to riddle Michael with bullets, sending him down a conveniently located nearby mine shaft.

In terms of characters, without Jamie Lee Curtis returning, the only one to come back is Donald Pleasence as Loomis. His character feels a little closer to that of the first film. He's still obsessive and erratic, but perhaps not as impulsive with his gun here. There's even a point where he tries to just talk to Michael and reason with him.

The most prominent new character is Ellie Cornell as Rachel. After the death of her parents, Jamie is taken care of by a foster family, the

Carruthers, and forms a close bond with their teenage daughter, Rachel. Outside of Jamie, she takes on the de facto Final Girl role of the movie, basically filling the void of the absent Laurie Strode.

The final scene of the film seems to set things up for another entry, having little Jamie taken over by the evil and killing her adoptive mother, much to Loomis's anguish. The scene is a complete recreation of the introduction of the first film, with Jamie dressed in the clown costume and the use of the POV shooting through the mask holes. It's clear that they were ready to continue the series, either with Michael returning as the villain, or Jamie taking on the role.

Part 4 was released right before Halloween, in a fairly competition-free weekend, and took the top spot, pulling in close to $7 million and going on to reach close to $18 million in its total run.[4] Although the budget had increased to a meatier $5 million, this still represented a healthy profit and the film was deemed a hit. Not quite the level of hit that the first one was, but enough for them to continue the series.

Although reviews for the film were once again overwhelmingly unfavorable, audiences were thrilled to see Michael Myers back in action, and many consider the film to be one of the best in the series. Some fans see it as a sort of reboot, considering how different it feels in tone, playing as a more straightforward slasher film of the era. It can be seen as the first entry of the "Jamie saga" as opposed to the earlier (and later) focus on Laurie.

With the franchise back in full swing, it only took one year until 1989's *Halloween 5: The Revenge of Michael Myers* hit the theaters. The production was considered rushed, with Akkad trying to strike while the property was once again hot.

Initially, Jeff Burr was in talks to take on the next entry, early in his career. Although he would go on to direct horror sequels for the *Texas Chainsaw Massacre, Stepfather,* and *Pumpkinhead* series, at this point he was still an untested entity. But before a deal could be signed, Debra Hill recommended the French-Swiss filmmaker Dominique Othenin-Girard, who had impressed her with his film *Night Angel.* Akkad quickly gave him the job and moved to get a script settled.

Because of the cliffhanger of the last film, the original script focused on Jamie becoming evil, while at the same time the Shape would continue to hunt after her, but Akkad decided against this avenue, claiming that audiences would want the movie to center around Michael, having learned his lesson from *Season of the Witch.* Another early script version did put the focus back onto Myers, but took an extremely unusual path in doing so. This version began right where the last one left off, with the killer at the bottom of the mine shaft. Then, similar to the revival of Jason, Michael would be struck by a bolt of lightning, returning him from the dead. The catch here is that the lightning would have purged him of his evil, and he would take on a more "misunderstood monster" role. He would still kill, but it would be in self-defense as people attacked him, considering that he was still a murderer at large. He would then seek out Loomis, who would attempt to help Michael and protect him from the angry mob of townspeople, although the film would once again end in his demise. Understandably, this version was also turned down. So the film went through another draft, bringing back young Jamie, this time downplaying the dark aspect, revealing that she didn't kill her foster mom, just attacked her, and has been rendered mute since. She's under the care of Loomis, and it's stated that one year has passed in between the two films, keeping us in real time and setting the film in 1989.

It's revealed that Michael survived the ending of the last film, falling into a river at the base of the mine shaft and being carried away. He's found and nursed back to health by an old hermit, although it should be noted that there's a lost segment in which he was instead rescued by a member of the Cult of Thorn, a story element that will resurface in the next film. The scene was reshot with the hermit when Akkad wanted to avoid the supernatural element, at least ... for now. Somehow, a strange rune tattoo is visible on Michael's wrist, which was not seen before, even in shots where his arms were visible. The purpose of this tattoo remains undiscussed in this film.

Apparently, Michael had been in the hermit's lair for the entire year, comatose, but he reawakens around spooky season, and here's where we get one of the odder continuity gaps. When he puts on his mask, which the hermit had conveniently just kept sitting beside the bed, it has completely changed. The look of it has dramatically shifted into a much narrower, angrier look. The lips and eyebrows are arched and more defined, and the neck is far more ill fitting, flaring out around the bottom. There is also a point in the film in which Michael trades in his mask for another. After killing off one of the random teenagers, he takes his mask in order to pose as him. It's a very different style of mask, way more defined than his standard Shatner, but was still just a repurposed mask that was readily available on the mass market. Referred to as the Brute mask, it is an exaggerated man's face with distorted features and short, shaggy hair. It can only be seen for the one segment of the film, before Michael switches back to his pale favorite.

There's also a bit of a timeline gaffe involving Jamie, although a minor one. In *Halloween 4*, there is a line of dialogue establishing Michael's niece as being seven years old, yet in this film, there are

Part 5 Michael's (Don Shanks) weird mask shape (with Donald Pleasance) (*Halloween 5: The Revenge of Michael Myers*, Magnum/Trancas, 1989).

multiple mentions of her being nine. This probably wouldn't be that big of an issue if the films both didn't take place right around Halloween, placing them pretty exactly one year apart. But it's not too big an error, and can be ascribed to rounding up or down when referring to her age.

The biggest break in continuity is the Myers house. After being absent from the third film, of course, and also not appearing in the fourth, we get a return visit to the house where it all started, and it's apparently had a bit of a renovation. In the story, Loomis uses Jamie as bait to lure Michael out into the open, taking her back to the killer's own childhood home. When we see it, however, gone is the simple suburban facade that was featured in the first two films. Instead, it's replaced by a large, dilapidated Victorian-style house, far removed from its modest original form. The reasoning for this is the change of shooting locations. The original two films were shot in South Pasadena, just outside of Los Angeles. *Halloween 5* was done in Salt Lake City, Utah, and going back to the original location for one shot was cost prohibitive, so they just found another house and went with it, I guess figuring that no one would notice. We did.

There would actually be a number of returning characters here, although the only one from the original entries would again be Dr. Loomis, once again played by Donald Pleasence. This film, however, portrays him in a far different light, going even further with his reckless obsessiveness than *Halloween II*. He frequently shouts at Jamie, trying to force her to help him to locate Michael, and at one point even uses her as bait in an effort to catch him. It's certainly a darker turn for the character, painting him in a far less heroic light than before. Danielle Lloyd would also return to play Jamie, and her character would also undergo a pretty drastic change, although a more motivated one. After her encounter in the last film, she will no longer speak, and has become more withdrawn. Rachel returns as well, in one of the more lamented story points, as her character is killed off early in the film. Audiences were upset that she was portrayed as a strong survivor in the previous film, yet is easily and quickly dispatched here, and the Final Girl focus is instead handed to a new character named Tina. Tina is pretty overwhelmingly hated by the fan base due to her grating, over-the-top personality.

A big element that is added in this film, perhaps its largest contribution to the overall lore of the story, is the confirmation of a psychic link between Michael and Jamie. Although it was hinted at in the last film, in this one it is explicitly shown. Jamie is able to see through Michael's eyes and detect his whereabouts, and vice versa. It's possibly the first concrete depiction of a supernatural occurrence in the entire series.

The film's finale is where the most contributions to the overall storyline come into play. Near the end, we get an uncharacteristically tender moment between Michael and Jamie, in which the Shape removes his mask and sheds a single tear. We briefly see his face, although it's in shadow, and details are hard to make out. He is played by a different actor here, of course, although he does look similar to when we last saw him. Oddly, he does not seem to be massively burned, although there does appear to be some possible scarring on his face. Apparently, much like Loomis, he must have gotten off a little easier than it appeared at the end of the second film. This doesn't really match up with him having to wear bandages on his face, ten years later, in the last film. The burns were extensive enough that his skin had to remain wrapped for ten years, but mild enough that they only left minor scars. Also, there is a close-up of his tear-filled eye, which appears to be intact, even though Laurie had placed bullets in both of them in the climax of that same film.

Then, Myers is captured by Loomis, who suffers a stroke in the process, and his fate is left uncertain. Michael's locked up in prison, where a mysterious man in black appears and destroys the police station, setting him free and then disappearing. We're once again left with a cliffhanger: our killer back on the loose, a mystery man helping him, Loomis possibly dead, and Jamie on her own, teeing things up for the series to continue.

One interesting thing to point out here is that the Man in Black was not part of the original script. The concept of a mystery man was actually devised about halfway through filming as a way to tie up some existing plot threads, while also creating a narrative device to carry forward into the following film. At the time, they just came up with the concept, with no actual clue as to who the Man in Black would eventually turn out to be. Othenin-Girard had theorized that the character could end up being an unrevealed twin brother of Michael's, or possibly a darker alter ego. Because of this, he had Don Shanks, the actor portraying Myers, perform the role. They also gave him a mysterious tattoo on his arm, the same tattoo that they had previously revealed on Michael.

Halloween 5 had an unexpectedly poor showing at the theaters, pulling in less than $12 million against a $5 million budget.[5] Comparatively, the fourth movie cost the same amount and yet earned close to $18 million, so Akkad decided to hold back with the series. The opening weekend was particularly humiliating since it was a Halloween-themed film release about two weeks before the holiday; somehow it didn't quite reach the number 1 spot, losing out to *Look Who's Talking*. And when I say that it lost out, I mean that it did less than half the business of a movie in which a talking baby had the voice of Bruce Willis.

Due to *Halloween 5*'s financial disappointment, Akkad decided to pump the brakes on the franchise, opting instead to figure out how to move forward with it. He felt that 5 strayed too far from the formula established in *Halloween 4*, leading to its failure, which was ironic considering one of the biggest criticisms of *Halloween 5* is that it feels remarkably similar to its predecessor and doesn't offer anything new.

It would take six years before the next entry, *Halloween: The Curse of Michael Myers* would see the light of day. In the gap between the movies, a series of complex legal issues would plague the franchise, as the rights would expire very shortly after release of *Halloween 5*. John Carpenter himself teamed up with New Line to try to get the rights, but lost out to Miramax/Dimension. So a new studio stepped in to handle things, and eventually started to get a script laid out.

The Curse of Michael Myers was a movie that seemed to be interested in both tying up whatever loose story threads that had been left unfulfilled, and starting up a new direction in order to distance itself from what was perceived as the staleness of the last entry. It was directed by Joe Chappelle, who would later go on to much larger success in television, having a big part in *The Wire* for HBO. Interestingly enough, John Carpenter was asked to return to the series in a writing role, but his proposal was scrapped since it involved sending Michael Myers to space. Akkad hated the idea, and sure, it sounds ridiculous, but is it really any sillier than how the film turned out? Another rejected script actually came from a pre-fame Quentin Tarantino, and it apparently bore an odd resemblance to his subsequent *Natural Born Killers*, as it was Michael and the Man in Black, cruising around Route 66 on a killing spree. There are conflicting reports about this, since Tarantino discusses writing the script, but others involved with the production state that he was never brought on in any sort of official capacity. It's theorized that after they had hired longtime Sam Raimi cohort Scott Spiegel to write and direct the film, he would go to Tarantino to handle the scripting issues for him, without ever being formally hired. Since Spiegel would eventually not end up directing, there was no further advancement on anything with their version.

The earliest version of the film was known as *Halloween 666: The Origin*, and it would introduce a new character named Dana Childress, a reporter plagued by dreams of Michael Myers, and would team up with Tommy Doyle, the little boy from the first film now grown up, to figure out why. Along the way, we would discover that Dr. Loomis has since been committed to a sanitarium, and that Dana is actually yet another secret sister of Myers. There are also several scenes involving VR for some reason, while also revealed that Michael is now living in a homeless shelter. Supposedly, after reading this version of the script, Akkad threw it across his office.

Eventually the script was finalized and production began, but all of the preproduction issues were just a drop in the bucket compared to the difficulties that were coming.

As far as continuity goes, it's kept pretty simple, since there's an opening narration that informs us that both Michael and Jamie have been missing for the past six years, since he escaped prison, giving us a pretty solid time frame and placing the film in 1995. There's actually a ton of linking to the previous films, as Jamie returns, but is considerably older now, presumably 15, and no longer played by Danielle Harris. She's pregnant and on the run, gives birth, and is shortly after caught and killed by Michael. But she's able to hide the baby beforehand, and it's rescued by another returning character, Tommy Doyle, the child that Laurie Strode was babysitting in the first film. He's played in this one by Paul Rudd, in the same year that he would also appear in the teen comedy, *Clueless*. Loomis is also back, and it's revealed that he not only survived his stroke, but also had plastic surgery (so that Donald Pleasence didn't have to sit in a makeup chair). They also bring back the character of Dr. Wynn, who appeared in one scene in the original film, a coworker and friend of Loomis, although also played by a new actor.

The Curse of Michael Myers plays it pretty loose with the overall series lore, introducing the concept of a group of druids called the Cult of Thorn that operates out of Haddonfield, who have been using Myers as their instrument. It seems that he's actually cursed with evil, and that curse can now be passed into Jamie's child, which is ... yeah ... that's a lot. There's also the introduction of more of the Strode family, as Laurie's adoptive uncle and aunt are here with their clan, having moved into the old Myers house for some reason. Once again, due to filming locations, the house has once again completely changed, and has been completely restored in the six years between the previous film and this one.

Michael's look remains basically the same, although once again, the mask has changed. This one is actually closer in design to the first film, becoming rounder, with a blanker expression and neater hair. It's usually considered one of the best looks out of all the sequels.

Although the film would include several returning characters, once again the only actor to reprise their role was Donald Pleasence. Besides the cosmetic change of the plastic surgery, the character would undergo a personality upgrade. In contrast to his manic, obsessive actions of *Halloween 5*, he instead takes on a more compassionate, calm demeanor. He still retains a strong interest in finding and capturing Michael, but seems more resigned to using traditional methods to do so.

The recasting of Jamie Lloyd would be one of the film's most egregious flaws, as many fans saw Danielle Harris as the character, and having another actress fill in just didn't work. Harris wasn't even considered for the role, mainly due to issues with money. For one thing, they didn't

Michael (George P. Wilbur) sports a return to classic stylings (*Halloween: The Curse of Michael Myers*, Miramax, 1995).

want to pay her any more than she had previously received for her role in *Halloween 4*, but more than that, Miramax wanted to skirt child labor laws. Since Harris was only 17 years old at the time, there was a very limited number of hours that she would be allowed on set. Akkad still wanted to include her in the role, and convinced her to emancipate from her parents in order to get around the regulations. She did this, but then discovered that in the newest version of the script, her character would be murdered within the first act of the film. Harris took offense to way her death was being handled and tried to negotiate, to no avail, so she walked away from the part.

Along the way, the mystery at the heart of the last film's cliffhanger would be resolved. The Man in Black is revealed to be none other than Dr. Wynn, who is not only evil, but the actual head of the Cult of Thorn. It is then insinuated that it was actually Wynn who assisted in Michael's escape in the first film, setting off the entire chain of events.

Another very minor and interesting bit of series continuity is the inclusion of a character named Mrs. Blankenship. She is introduced here as a member of the Cult, and revealed to have been a young Michael's babysitter, helping to shape his evil. This is notable due to the fact that there is reference to a character named Minnie Blankenship in *Halloween III: Season of the Witch*. At one point in that film, one of the main characters states that her father had an appointment with Mrs. B., who would have worked at the villainous Silver Shamrock Novelties. This creates the possibility that the two films could take place in the same universe, sharing a continuity. The fact that Dr. Challis is watching the original film on TV creates a bit of issue with that, but it could be possible to explain that away. It would make some sort of sense to have the characters linked, since it's revealed that the Blankenship of *The Curse of Michael Myers* is a member of the Druid cult, while Minnie Blankenship of *Halloween III* works for the evil company that is also run by some sort of Druidic cult.

The ending of the film is probably one of the most confusing of the entire series, mainly for external reasons. In the theatrical release, the ending features a showdown with Michael and the future Ant-Man that ends with Tommy stabbing the killer with a green liquid, seemingly killing him. Afterward, Loomis goes back in to make sure that Michael is finally dead, and we're left with a shot of the mask on the ground, and the good doctor screaming in the background. We're never shown what he's reacting to, and the fate of both characters is unknown, leaving a cliffhanger for a future entry. But this isn't how it was supposed to end. Before release, a test audience hated the movie and there were reshoots and re-edits to try to pull together a more audience-friendly version.

Because of this, several elements were altered, key subplots were deleted, and an entirely new ending was created. In this version, Tommy uses the Druids' magic against them, using runes to trap Michael, instead of having a physical fight. Here, when Loomis goes back in, he finds Myers on the ground and removes his mask, only to see Wynn there instead, mocking him and giving him the Thorn curse on his arm. Our final shot is Michael walking away, now dressed in the garb of the Man in Black. It's pretty easy to see why they changed it, since it leans a little harder into the whole supernatural aspect of things, but the problem came when Donald Pleasence passed away before they did the reshoots. Because of this, they had to shoot and cut around his character, and constructed the vague final scene of the released version, although let's face it: neither version really makes much sense. As a quick note, the producer's cut of the film also has a title card at the beginning explicitly stating the year as 1995.

Oh, yeah, about that producer's cut. It contains quite a bit of variation from the released version, but one of its most obvious changes is possibly one of the more controversial elements of the film. Remember earlier when I said that Jamie was pregnant? Well, in the producer's cut, it's heavily implied that the father of that baby was none other than Michael himself. The identity of the child's father is never really addressed in the actual film, and it seems that an early version of the script stated that Wynn had raped Jamie, leading to the pregnancy, although that is never stated nor implied in the finished product. Based on some of the equipment in Wynn's lab, including several dead fetuses, it could also be taken that the child was the product of artificial insemination. Considering none of this is confirmed by the film, and the producer's cut is considered the non-canon version of events, it is still up to the discretion of the viewer. It should be noted, however, that the official *Halloween* wiki does state that baby Steven is Michael's son through the process of cloning. They went the less gross route.

Screenwriter Daniel Farrands would actually state that there were several other endings that were planned, with no decisions being made about the actual finale until just before shooting. Some of these included one in which Michael slashes Loomis's throat; one in which Danny, the little boy character of the film, inherited the evil and would then kill his mother; and one in which Wynn is blown up by a bomb in a helicopter.

The Curse of Michael Myers didn't seem to affect the box office, since it outperformed the previous entry by a good margin. Also made on a $5 million budget, it earned $15 million total in its theatrical run, placing it between the takes of the fourth and fifth films. Its opening weekend was pretty notable, since it did over $7 million, which was the highest since the second film,[6] and it was only outperformed by the box office powerhouse, *Se7en*. Even though the profit margin was enough to continue the franchise, it was decided that the current series direction wasn't really resonating with fans, and a rather bold reinvention was needed. Audiences wanted that classic paradox of horror sequels: something new and different, but also kinda the same.

A mere three years after *The Curse of Michael Myers*, the next entry would bring with it a new air of respectability and a complete disregard for what had come before it, changing the course of horror sequels forever.

To celebrate the 20th anniversary of the first film, with 1998 came the release of *Halloween H20: 20 Years Later*. This one actually took several drafts to reach the final product, with early concepts for the film being a direct sequel to *The Curse of Michael Myers*, with Tommy Doyle once again the main character continuing his fight against the Cult of Thorn. This version was also written by Daniel Farrands, and sported the title *Michael Myers: Lord of the Dead*. Not much is known about this particular treatment, except that it included the whole town being part of the cult. There was another draft that was pitched by Robert Zappia, entitled *Two Faces of Evil*. His version involved Michael returning to life again, this time causing chaos at the boarding school that Laurie was said to have attended. It's a pretty standard entry, save for the unusual story element of another serial killer that is being used by police to help them track and capture Michael, in the vein of *Silence of the Lambs*. There is very little continuity in this draft, and only a few passing mentions to the prior entries, and it was quickly discarded. It wasn't until Jamie Lee Curtis expressed interest in returning to the role of Laurie that the film started to take shape, forever changing the course of the series' history.

The studio saw a chance to bring the franchise back in a big way and tapped Kevin Williamson to deliver a version of the script. At the time, his career was white hot due to the success of the *Scream* series and *I Know What You Did Last Summer*, and having his name attached to a project brought as much clout as a returning Jamie Lee. Williamson's first shot at the concept actually kept in continuity with the original six films. He intended to bring Laurie back, and reveal that she had faked her death in order to hide from Michael, an element that is carried over into the finished film. However, in the original version, it happened in the same universe in which the fourth, fifth, and sixth films occurred. At one point, she finds out that her daughter, Jamie, has been killed by Myers, and has a moment of mourning. This take on it does slightly diminish the character of Laurie, considering that she essentially abandoned her daughter, leaving her to fend for herself in three differ-ent attacks by the killer, with the third one ultimately taking her life. In order to reflect its place in the series, the original working title was *Hal-loween 7: The Revenge of Laurie Strode*. It should be noted that William-son didn't actually complete a full script and only worked on story ideas and concepts for the film, as well as some dialogue touch-ups. His work didn't get him a writer's credit, but he did merit a "story by" tag.

With Curtis's return, there was an attempt to bring Carpenter back on board as well, and surprisingly, the auteur was interested. However, the director was still unhappy with how his share of the profits from the first film were handled, so he increased his standard fee. Instead of his regular price of $10 million, he also demanded a three-picture deal with Dimension. This stipulation proved to be a little too pricey for Akkad, so the negotiations ended. Instead, Steve Miner, director of *Friday the 13th Part 2* and *Part III*, came on board. At this point in his career, he had mostly left horror behind, with his most recent works actually being family friendly comedies, and *H20* would serve as his grand return to the genre.

The biggest and most notorious element of this entry is the total continuity reboot. At some point in the development process, it was decided that the anniversary film, which didn't have a sequel number attached to the end, would ignore everything outside of the first two films. The third through sixth films would be erased from continuity. This allowed them to get around the fact that Laurie Strode has been killed off in *Halloween 4*, without having to acknowledge the baggage that the previous three films had brought. Because of this, the last time the audience would have seen these versions of the characters was the ending of *Halloween II*. We were reset once again to a Laurie that had survived a grueling night against her murderous brother, and a Michael and Loomis that barely survived a massive fire. Everything else, includ-ing Jamie Lloyd, the Cult of Thorn, and saucy Tommy Doyle, had been erased.

In terms of the film's timeline, it once again is kind enough to just let us know where it lands, with an opening card that places it in 1998, so it's also set on the 20th anniversary of the first one. Any time a movie flashes that big ol' time stamp on the screen is a big plus for me, since it makes the timeline guy's job about three hundred times easier.

The first revelation is that, similar to the previous timeline, Sam Loomis managed to survive the explosion at the end of the film, and continued his search for Michael. Since Donald Pleasence had passed on, he's not seen in the movie, but the character's voice is heard and pictures are shown as the character has also recently died. It's a little unusual that they indicate that Sam had survived the second film, only to have him die later on, instead of just having him die in the fire, but perhaps it's a remnant of the earlier draft which maintained the series continuity. In another nice nod to the earlier films, Marion Chambers, the nurse who was with Loomis the night Michael escaped, returns, although she is killed early on. She is once again played by Nancy Stephens, reprising the role after for the first time since *Halloween II*.

We also discover that Laurie Strode is indeed alive, and has changed her name and identity and is now heading up a private school that her teenage son attends. John is turning 17, which means that he was born just a few years after the events of the second film. In this version of the story, instead of Michael being comatose after the hospital fire, he's just been missing. How he survived the blaze, and what he has been doing in the interim, is never revealed. After 20 years, on the eve of John's 17th birthday, Michael reemerges to once again begin his family stalking. It's established that he knows of Laurie's son and her current whereabouts from going through Loomis's files after killing Nurse Chambers. This does create an odd logic issue, since it's insinuated that he's back on the hunt for Laurie after all this time because it coincides with her son turning the same age that she was in their first encounter. But it's also implied that he learns of the son from these files, which would be an odd coincidence. The only explanation for it is that Michael was aware she had a son a very long time ago, decided to lie in wait until his 17th birthday, and merely needed the file to obtain her present whereabouts. This doesn't necessarily explain exactly why Loomis would maintain a file on a patient who had faked her death that included all the details of her false identity—that would seem to defeat the purpose of a false identity—but let's face it. We've already established that Sam Loomis wasn't necessarily the best and most thoughtful of doctors.

The look of the Shape is again a source of discontinuity, and was also a source of behind-the-scenes drama. For some reason, it seems like the most difficult aspect of Michael's ensemble to pin down is the general look of the mask, as we've discussed already. This film is no better and features no fewer than four different designs. There's the main mask, used for the bulk of the film, which is much more detailed and sculpted, with eyebrows and frizzy hair. This mask was a last-minute addition, as there was a previous mask that was used for the bulk of the shoot. This mask is very unique, with much wider eye holes and a pug nose, giving it a more expressive look. The hair was longer, and pulled back. Unfortunately, after looking at footage, the producers absolutely hated this mask, and went back to reshoot using the other design. Also unfortunately, one of the sets was no longer available to shoot on, so

Michael (Chris Durand) displays the infamous CGI mask (with Adam Hann-Byrd) (*Halloween H20: 20 Years Later,* Miramax, 1998).

instead of reshooting, they just placed a CGI mask overtop of the existing image, and it remains visible for one shot. Finally, in the beginning scenes, the main mask was apparently still in the process of being created, so they substituted in a mask from the sixth film, which is visible in several shots.

Most of the action takes place in the boarding school, details of which are built off the earlier draft from Zappia. Outside of the returning Laurie, and the introduction of her son John, the cast is rounded out by the teen boy's school friends. Foremost among these is his girlfriend, Molly, played by Academy Award nominee Michelle Williams. She had just recently come into prominence on the television show *Dawson's Creek,* another of Williamson's projects, after acting in several projects as a child actor, but *H20* would serve as one her first larger-scale film roles. There was also a comic relief element, provided by LL Cool J as the school's security guard.

H20 ends in a pretty definitive manner, with Laurie having a final head-to-head with her brother, pinning him to a tree in a car wreck, and finally using an axe to chop off his head. This would seem to be a pretty clear death for the character, and end the series, but I don't even have to finish this sentence for you to know that it clearly did not. On an interesting note, the film does not hint at a sequel, although one was planned anyway. Akkad actually had a clause in the contract stating that Michael Myers could not conclusively be killed off, which frustrated Jamie Lee Curtis, who wanted the series to end. The topic was heated enough that at one point, Curtis was ready to leave the project unless the film ended definitively with no setups for further films. A compromise was reached when screenwriter Kevin Williamson wrote an ending in which Michael switched places with a paramedic, allowing him to be killed in his place, and it was filmed, but not used in the film, instead being saved for use in a sequel. This gave them a scenario in which Michael is not actually killed off, even though it's not seen on-screen. Curtis agreed to this on the condition that this ending would not be discussed at the time of *H20*'s release.

Obviously, this film being a higher profile, with a return for the series in terms of star power, expectations were high. As such, it was given a bigger budget to work with, adding up to $17 million, with a solid $5 million of that going to Jamie Lee Curtis. All of this led to a healthy amount of hype leading up to the film's August release. A summer berth was unusual for the series, as opposed to coming out around Halloween time, and represented yet another gamble. It paid off, since it debuted to a $16 million weekend, earning back almost its entire production cost in the first three days. Although it only reached the number 3 spot, mainly due to the competition of the juggernaut of *Saving Private Ryan* and the Nic Cage action flick, *Snake Eyes*. But considering those films both had budgets north of $70 million, the relatively lower-cost horror film was considered a huge success. It collected a total of $55 million in its run, matching that of *Snake Eyes*, creating an interesting analysis.[7] That film would be considered a disaster, losing quite a bit of money, whereas *Halloween* would be noted as a big hit, earning several times its budget.

Critics were marginally kinder to this episode as well, as Rotten Tomatoes currently shows it with a 52 percent positive ranking from critics. At the time of release, it had quite a bit of love from fans of the series, although time has softened that perspective, with the current view being that it's a merely acceptable entry, perhaps better than the few that came before it, but still a pale shadow of the original.

As stated before, the intentions of making another entry had been made clear well before the success of *H20*, and preproduction began pretty quickly afterward. Akkad wanted to strike while the iron was hot, but one thing that wasn't counted on was the difficulty in finding a workable script.

There were several failed attempts, including a rather notorious one by a returning Daniel Farrands, reusing that lost title, *Halloween 8: Lord of the Dead*. It was an attempt to resolve the continuity issues and actually tied *H20* back into the former timeline. The story brought back Tommy Doyle from the sixth film, on the run from the law, teaming up with Lindsay Wallace, another character from the original film. The pair would be dealing with a returning Michael seemingly back from the dead after being decapitated, while poring through Loomis's old files. Half of the film would be a flashback to Myers's youth, delving into the evil developing within him, while the other half would deal with Doyle and Wallace being attacked in the present day. In the finale, the killer would be unmasked, only to reveal an insane Laurie as the stalker, taking up the mantle from her brother. Although this version was discarded, it was later adapted into a comic book series from Chaos Comics.

Ultimately, the task of writing the new film would go to Sean Hood and the late Larry Brand. Normally, being handed the job of picking up a series after the main antagonist just had their head chopped off would be something of a difficult task. But the heavy lifting of figuring out how to get out of that situation had already been handled by Williamson, so it was just a matter of figuring out where to go from there.

The next episode in the saga picks up where *H20* left off, running with the continuity that film established instead of the former series. Although technically *Halloween 8*, it was released in 2002 as *Halloween: Resurrection*, possibly the most infamous in the entire run.

Jamie Lee Curtis once again appeared, with many reservations. She was pretty ready to be done with the franchise, but there was a clause in her contract stipulating that she would return in another entry if one were to be greenlit. She agreed to do so, under one condition: that Laurie Strode would be killed off once and for all.

Curtis wasn't the only returning member of a previous production, as Rick Rosenthal, who directed *Halloween II*, stepped back in to lead up this one. Dwight Little, the director of *Halloween 4*, had been offered the role, but turned it down, clearing the way for Rosenthal to return to the chair.

It's established early on that Michael did indeed survive the finale of the last film, and Laurie has been institutionalized for accidentally killing an innocent man, the paramedic. One of the doctors there lets us know that the events of the last film took place three years ago, and it's once again Halloween, so we're set in October 2001. The real Michael has been missing since then, but finally comes out of hiding to attack his sister, finally killing her off. Laurie is not only stabbed, but is then thrown off of a rooftop to the ground below, giving her a pretty final demise. Or as final as any death in a horror film can be. As we'll soon see, Laurie will return just a short while later.

After finally ending his family line, Michael returns home to the Myers house, which has once again gone through a drastic overhaul. Again, the shooting locations were completely different, so the exterior of the house once again changes. It's old and dilapidated and somehow reverts closer to its original appearance, although you never get a direct view of it in the film. Since this entry was shot in Canada, they didn't have access to the original house to use, so they actually constructed it on a set. As a result of the reboot, this would be the first time seeing the house since *Halloween II* in this version of the timeline, and the later residences shown in the other movies have been erased.

Since everything from this particular era of filmmaking had to somehow involve the internet, a web show is there, filming a live event, and Michael begins to indiscriminately murder them. Busta Rhymes is here as the showrunner, and ultimately ends up being Myers's prime opponent, but there's plenty of other cannon fodder to run through, including *Battlestar Galactica*'s Katee Sackhoff, and a small role for Tyra Banks.

From a continuity standpoint, it doesn't change too much, outside of the house's appearance. Except for the introduction with Laurie, there's very little in the rest of the film to link to the others, especially since most of them don't officially exist anymore. The character of John is only mentioned in passing and his ultimate fate is unrevealed.

The look of Michael has changed yet again, with another redesign of the trademark mask. This time, however, listening to criticism of the look of the last films, they went back to a styling closer to that of the original film. The *Resurrection* mask is often considered one of the better looks of the sequels, but it does differ from the original slightly. It's more expressive, with the facial features more detailed and eyebrows clearly defined. No explanation is given for the variation of his mask in the film. It could be theorized that he found a new one in the gap between films, but in the flashbacks to the end of the previous entry, he's shown to be wearing this mask instead, creating a minor continuity error.

This one's ending isn't as definite as the previous one, as Michael is karate-kicked and then electrocuted, but at the end is shown to still be

A more expressive and defined look for Michael (Brad Loree with Busta Rhymes) (*Halloween: Resurrection*, Miramax, 2002).

alive and ready for more. I guess I should state that one more time for emphasis: Michael is karate-kicked by Busta Rhymes, who then delivers a James Bond–style post-kill one-liner.

Unfortunately, unlike the warm reception for *H20*, this film's reception wasn't so glowing; it was critically trounced, and also hated by fans. People trashed everything from the haphazard way of explaining away the last film's ending to the focus on internet culture, the killing off of Laurie, and the comic relief of Rhymes.

Like its predecessor, it was given a summer release, and was up against some stiff competition. It debuted at number 4, with an opening weekend of $12 million, and while that was still somewhat respectable considering the modest $15 million budget, the post opening drop-off was considerable. It only pulled in around $38 million in total, a little more than half of that of *H20*, and is widely considered to be one of the worst in the series.[8] Given the return to the profit margins of the fifth and sixth entries, it seemed like the franchise might be dead, and in need of zombification.

For the next couple of years, several further installments were developed, but none reached fruition. They ranged from a prequel, set in the period between *Halloween II* and *H20*, to one that focused on John Tate getting his revenge on Michael for killing his mother, to another that brought back the character of Jamie Lloyd, to a crossover between *Halloween* and *Hellraiser* in which Michael is revealed to have received his supernatural strength and durability from the Lament Configuration. It's crazy to think how close this last project came to happening—it was only killed off by an online poll in which 52 percent of respondents said they would not be interested in it.

After several years of no motion within the series, tragedy of another kind entirely struck, revealing a real-life horror story. Moustapha Al Akkad, longtime producer of the series and driving force behind the franchise, was in Amman, Jordan, with his daughter. They were both in the lobby of their hotel, a Grand Hyatt, when it was the subject of a terrorist attack. It was one of three attacks on several hotels, and a total of 57 people were killed. Akkad's daughter died instantly in the blast, and he died a mere two days later, in the hospital. With his death, his son, Malek, took over the producing role for the franchise and decided that it was time to take Michael in a different direction.

It was around this time that the *Texas Chainsaw Massacre* remake had done gangbuster business, so everyone was jumping on the bandwagon of rebooting their own franchises. The decision was made to once again reset Michael Myers's continuity with a full-blown remake, headed up by Rob Zombie.

When it comes to continuity, *Halloween* (2007) is a complete restart for the series, and once again erases previous events. This time, however, instead of eliminating everything except the first two films, it discards everything and starts completely fresh. Unlike the first movie, this version goes further into the Myers family psychology, establishing that Michael's upbringing was difficult, with a stripper mother and an abusive stepfather. He's established to be mentally disturbed even before killing his sister, giving a backstory that many felt was unnecessary to the character. However, this new look into the character was essential for Zombie, who felt that familiarity had softened Michael's image, and that audiences no longer found him scary. In his opinion, delving further into the reasoning behind his motivations would restore him to his frightening glory. It was an unusual move, considering that most viewers found the lack of motive to actually be the scariest thing about Myers in the first place.

Over the course of the film, we meet our new Laurie and Loomis, although their characters have been altered as well, making them angrier and more unlikable than before, as every single one of Zombie's characters is written as if they came from the same broken home. After the first half of the film, which is mostly new and original material fleshing out the background of the characters, the second half would instead play out in much the same way as the original, feeling more like a traditional remake.

The role of Michael had been filled by a variety of actors, but this marked the first time in which he was played by a known entity, as opposed to a stuntman. The part was played by Tyler Mane, professional wrestler, who had previously made a name in the film industry by playing Sabertooth in the first *X-Men* movie. As compared to previous portrayals of the character, Mane was noticeably much larger. In this version, Michael is a virtual mountain of a man, looking more in form like Jason Voorhees than his own earlier forms. He's also shown to be significantly more violent here, with most of his kills being more savage and aggressive.

It's also the first time that we hear Michael speak, albeit only in his younger form. Since a portion of this film takes place when he is younger, and prior to the murder of his sister, he is played by child actor Daeg Faerch. In this one, instead of just killing his older sibling, he also murders a bullying classmate, his sister's boyfriend, and his mother's trashy boyfriend.

The look of Michael actually changes quite a bit over the film's runtime. Instead of the clown costume from the original, he conducts the first set of killings while wearing the standard Shatner-inspired mask.

Due to his age, it is oversized and ill fitting. After the opening sequence of events, and the film's shift to a grown Michael, he is first seen wearing a standard uniform for the Smith's Grove patients and a makeshift, papier-mâché mask. He remains in this look for a while, gaining his traditional jumpsuit from a trucker that he kills along the way. Finally, after making his way back to his childhood home, he retrieves the white mask from beneath the floorboards, at last looking the part. The mask is incredibly accurate to that of the original film—it's often considered one of the best of the series—and is differentiated by its cracked and weathered appearance, due to being hidden away for so long.

The role of Loomis is filled with yet another genre veteran with Malcolm McDowell, perhaps best known as *A Clockwork Orange*'s Alex the Droog, stepping into the role. McDowell's take on the character is far more cynical, with him being far more interested in how to leverage his work with Michael into a book deal and celebrity status. That being said, his version does end up appearing to be slightly more competent than his predecessor in that his negligence is due to his own personal callousness, instead of just general ineptitude. In short, this version of Loomis doesn't set off events that cause an innocent teenage to be run over by a car and burned alive. Although, that being said, it is his book that reveals the true identity of Michael's sister, who had been given a new name to distance her from the scandal with her family.

Laurie is played by Scout Taylor-Compton, who had been in a series of television appearances and small film roles, but this represented her first major part in a feature. Her version of Laurie is slightly less wholesome, coming off as more argumentative and combative with her friends, which is a Zombie trademark.

Several other roles are filled by horror vets, including Chucky

The remake's cracked-up look as Michael (Tyler Mane) returns home (with Dee Wallace) (*Halloween*, the Weinstein Company/Dimension, 2007).

himself (Brad Dourif) portraying Sheriff Brackett, William Forsythe, literal human skull Richard Lynch, Udo Kier, Machete himself Danny Trejo, Clint Howard, Chop Top Bill Moseley, and *Police Academy*'s Leslie Easterbrook. To cap it off, in a fun bit of homage to the franchise, former Jamie Lloyd portrayer Danielle Harris is cast as this version's Annie Brackett.

From a timeline perspective, it's a difficult film to pin down, since the opening prologue appears to be set in the 1970s, judging from the clothing, cars, and technology. The original script apparently set those events in 1978, the year of the original film's release, but the released version never specifies. We're told that there's a 17-year gap while Michael is locked away, and although that would set it in 1995, there are current tech phones and autos featured, and it looks to be set in the year of release, making it 2007, with the earlier scenes being set in 1990.

The ending of the film is another curious conundrum, since two different versions exist. The standard version, seen in theaters, ends with Laurie and Loomis facing off with Michael at the Doyle house. Here, Myers tussles with the doctor, possibly killing him, although it's unclear, with Laurie and the killer ending up falling out of a window to the sidewalk below. There, the Final Girl takes Loomis's gun and aims it at Michael's head, firing, although there's a possibility that the killer's hand deflects the shot. The finality of it is unresolved. But in the original ending, which would be restored later in the director's cut of the film, Myers gets ahold of Strode outside the house, surrounded by police officers. The doc is able to get through to Michael by talking to him, and he releases his victim. Immediately after, the police open fire on Myers, killing him in a rain of gunfire. This ending seems a little more final than the theatrical version, but it's a horror movie, so either way they went, there would be a way forward.

Even with a higher-profile, buzz-worthy director, a collection of known names, and a fresh start for the series, the budget was kept to a modest $15 million, comparable to that of *H20* and *Resurrection*. It seemed as if the film was handed an extra challenge when a version of the workprint was leaked on the internet. There were concerns that easy access to viewing the film at home for free would damage the box office performance, but Zombie quickly addressed it by stating that the leaked version was dramatically different than what would be seen in theaters. In any case, it didn't really seem to matter, as the film did quite well. It was released over Labor Day weekend, against minimal competition. Over the four days, it managed to bring in just over $30 million, breaking the weekend's previous record of $20 million, and would hold that title all the way until 2021. After doubling its budget in one weekend, it would then go on to amass a total of around $80 million worldwide, becoming the highest-grossing entry in the franchise at the time.[9]

Unsurprisingly, critics once again had general distaste for the film, although there was one particular opinion that stood out a little more than others. John Carpenter, although showing a small amount of appreciation for the film, has been on record stating that he didn't really care for the expansion of Michael's backstory, feeling it took away from the villain's mystique.

After the massive success of the film, it would appear as if a sequel was a given, although Rob Zombie himself wasn't so keen on the idea. Immediately after the film's release, he stated that he felt burned out, and not interesting in helming the sequel. Because of this Akkad began to court the French directing team of Julien Maury and Alexandre Bustillo, who had just gained acclaim with their film *Inside*. However, after a year passed, and Zombie's burnout faded, he became more open to the idea, so it looked as if another entry would soon arrive.

Two years later, in 2009, it did with *Halloween II*. Pretty much the entire cast would return for the follow-up, which drastically diverged from the previous film to hold the name. If one of the primary criticisms of Zombie's first was that it too closely mirrored the original, this one would avoid that by being so different from anything that came before it. This was actually at the behest of Akkad, who was so excited to have the director back for the second entry that he told him that there were no rules. He could take the film in any direction that he wanted, and actually encouraged him to diverge from the series formula.

The first 20 minutes or so presents itself as a traditional reinterpretation of the original *Halloween II*, with Laurie recovering in the hospital while Michael attacks, although it's revealed to only be a dream. It almost feels as if this entire sequence was added in to give a feel of familiarity, something in common with the film whose name it is taking, before going off into a completely different realm.

Because at that point, the rest of the movie goes into totally different territory, establishing itself as being one year later, with our young heroine's life in shambles. So, if the last film mainly took place in 2007, then this would be one year later, in 2008.

As far as continuity goes, it's pretty consistent with the last film. Considering that both entries were written and directed by Zombie, and they were produced within a short amount of time, allowing for the full cast to return, there are no real drastic changes, outside of those pushed forward by the storyline. The one exception to this is the appearance of young Michael in flashbacks. In this film, both Michael and Laurie have visions of their mother, a white horse, and a youthful version of the killer. Because the actor who played him in the 2007 film had now aged beyond looking like the character, a new young man was cast to take his place.

Laurie's character represents a big shift from her presentation in the prior film, although a motivated one. Her experiences a year ago have left her emotionally damaged, lashing out at everyone around her. Her personality comes off even more like a standard Rob Zombie character, jumping straight into the pool of horribleness. This is a Laurie who is pretty difficult to root for, even considering the trauma she has been though.

This is made even more blatant by the presence of a returning Danielle Harris, with the revelation that her character survived her encounter with Michael. It could be argued that Annie's experiences were far more taxing than those of Laurie, yet she seems to be holding it together quite well, further making the portrayal of Laurie difficult to relate to.

Loomis's negative traits are also amplified here. He has also survived the events of the first film, and has released a book about his story, profiting heavily off of the events. His callousness is turned up, and he is played as an even greater cartoon character than before.

Once again, Zombie managed to work in small appearances by a number of cult actors, including *Texas Chainsaw Massacre 2*'s Stretch (Caroline Williams), the one true Lois Lane (Margot Kidder), Dr. Johnny Fever (Howard Hesseman), and, for some reason, "Weird" Al Yankovic.

The look of the Shape is the biggest variation from what came before, but again, not so much an error as one of an advancing plot. Michael's mask is now tattered and torn, with half of his face exposed. Underneath, his appearance is that of an unshaven, long-haired ball of dirt, causing fans to refer to him as Hobo Michael. The mask is basically the same as the one from the last film, except most of it is now gone. It's a pretty drastic overhaul for the aesthetic of the character, again played by Mane, matching the change in direction for the film overall.

This one ends on a fairly definitive note, with another big standoff between our three central characters. This time, Michael stabs Loomis and kills him, before being shot by police and then stabbed by Laurie. She then walks out into the open, wearing Michael's mask, and the ending seems to insinuate that she has either been taken over by the same evil that plagued Michael, or is possibly killed by the police.

The sequel did not reach the heights of its predecessor, pulling in less than $40 million at the box office. It was released a touch earlier than the previous film, and faced competition from another big horror franchise with *The Final Destination.* It opened at $16 million, and came in third place, which was not a good sign. Although the budget

H2's Hobo Michael (Tyler Mane with Malcolm McDowell) (*Halloween II,* the Weinstein Company/Dimension, 2009).

was again only $15 million, and this did represent a solid profit, it was still less than half of the haul that the first one achieved.[10] Plus, critical and audience reaction was solidly negative, showing a rapidly declining interested in Zombie's vision of the franchise. Or just Zombie's films in general. Take your pick.

Even given that, the Weinstein Company, who now held the rights to the characters, decided to move forward with it, which isn't surprising considering that the phrase "terrible decisions" and "Weinstein" go hand in hand. Even though Rob Zombie declined to return for a third part, they announced they were moving forward with a concept called *Halloween 3-D.* Miramax tapped the team of Patrick Lussier and Todd Farmer, who had just had some success with their remake of *My Bloody Valentine.* Their script would retcon the end of the last film to show that it was actually Laurie who killed Loomis, and that Michael wasn't even present for the finale. It also brings back Sheriff Brackett, only to have him killed off pretty early on. It then focuses on mostly new characters, and ends with Laurie being pretty definitively killed off, with Michael still at large. An interesting part of the script is that as opposed to the last film, this one would have Michael sporting a new version of his classic mask, replacing the cracked and torn one from before. However, late in the film, this mask would be removed, revealing the old mask underneath, burned onto his flesh by a fire during the first act. Ultimately, this version would be canceled due to Farmer and Lussier's prior commitment to another project, and the decision was made to go in an entirely different direction.

The next pass at the script would take a few years to make happen, but around 2015, it really looked like *Halloween Returns* was going to happen. Patrick Melton and Marcus Dunstan were hired to take a crack at the concept, and were handed a pretty difficult challenge. A decision had to be made whether to return to the original continuity, use the *H20* version of things, or continue in the remake universe. They took a completely different tactic, planning to once again have their film eliminate everything outside of the first two films. Their version would wipe away not only the fourth, fifth, and sixth films, but also everything that came after them. It would actually have been set 10 years after the original murders, with Michael still on death row after his rampage. Of course, he would escape, commencing an entirely new set of attacks. There's a decent amount of appreciation for the script online, saying that it harkens back to the feel of the original movie, but confusingly, given its "ten years later" setting, the film would feature smartphones and characters talking about taking selfies. Apparently, the intended idea was that the original film would be retconned to taking place in the mid–2000s, and the new film would take place in the modern day. There is very little mention of either Loomis or Laurie in it, instead focusing on new characters. But before this version could make it into production, Dimension lost the rights to the series, and it was also canceled.

It didn't take long for someone to snap them up, and Blumhouse Productions, along with Universal Pictures, acquired the rights in 2016. They had a different view of the direction of the series, as did John Carpenter, who was very unhappy with what had been done with Michael Myers in the last several movies. He realized that he had been extremely critical of all of the attempts to follow up his masterpiece and decided to put his money where his mouth was, and see if he could help restore the franchise to its former glory. When David Gordon Green and Danny McBride came aboard, they made a decision that would make everything make more sense, and yet be utterly confusing at the same time.

Instead of choosing to continue the Rob Zombie interpretation, or picking up where *Resurrection* left off, or even going back to the original timeline by continuing from *Curse*, they decided to reboot things once again. Similar to *H20* and the abandoned *Halloween Returns*, they proposed wiping out previous continuity. But instead of doing what had already been done before, they went one step further by eliminating the second film as well, making the original film the only existing piece of canon.

In 2018, 40 years after the first film, the latest, simply titled *Halloween*, was released, and followed through with that vision. The film picks up 40 years after that one fateful night, and the time frame is given several times, firmly placing the year as 2018. Instead of following Laurie to a hospital, Michael Myers was instead captured and placed in an institution, where he's been ever since.

Now, here's where things get a bit different. Because of the elimination of the first *Halloween II*, the plot point of Laurie being Michael's sister is also erased, and she is now just his surviving victim, still suffering from PTSD because of the incident. They chose to discard the family element of the storyline, realizing that the notion of being a random victim is scarier than being a targeted one. Because of this, Michael doesn't necessarily have a connection with Strode, outside of her just being a girl that he attacked four decades ago. Laurie has an estranged daughter, played by Judy Greer, and a granddaughter, who is approximately the same age that Laurie was in the original. In an early version of the script, her daughter was named Jamie, as an odd sort of homage to the original continuity. This was discarded pretty early on, and her name was changed to Karen. Of course, Loomis is absent, and his character has also passed on.

Due to the clean-slate approach, obviously continuity is not really an issue within this film, and the links between this and the first one work, as there are very few.

Jamie Lee Curtis obviously returned to the role of Laurie, a detail that the filmmakers were a bit concerned about. After all, she had previously declared that she was done with the character, and had herself killed off in *Resurrection*. That being said, after seeing the script and this version of the heroine, she quickly signed on. The depiction of Laurie is very different than we saw in the previous reboot, with her acting fractured and combative with those around her. She's distanced herself from her family, built a sort of fortress in the woods, and has issues with alcohol. It's a bit out of sorts, considering that they eliminated the second film, reducing her initial incident with Michael to a very short encounter that lasted all of about ten minutes, instead of two separate incidents over the course of an entire night. The concept that the encounter would still be such a prominent part of her life, 40 years later, is a little odd.

Curtis wasn't the only returning cast member; Nick Castle, the original Michael Myers, reprised the role. He doesn't portray the killer in every scene, sharing the role with stuntman James Jude Courtney, but reportedly does the majority of on-screen work.

Because of this, the depiction of Michael Myers is probably the most accurate and consistent with the original in the whole series. The mask is an almost perfect reproduction of the classic one, just more weathered and cracked with age. For the beginning of the film, he is seen without his Shatner mask for a few scenes, although always just out of view, but it's clear to see that there is some continuity with the wounds the character had suffered before, like his eye that is damaged from being stabbed with a coat hanger during the '78 version's closet scene. In this scene, his advanced age is apparent, as he would be 61 years old or so at this point.

Early in the film, an inmate transfer goes wrong, allowing Myers to escape captivity and once again go on his rampage. He is able to regain his original mask through a series of very coincidental circumstances. The day before, a couple of true crime podcasters stop by Smith's Grove to interview Michael, because the guest that everyone wants on their podcast is the guy who hasn't said a word in over 40 years. They somehow have gotten their hands on the mask and bring it with them to show him. After he escapes, the team is still in town and by pure happenstance run across the killer. He murders them, reclaiming his true face.

The interesting problem that comes across with this one is that Michael has no real connection to Laurie. He has no reason to seek her out, even though she appears convinced that he will. But with the elimination of the sister angle, Myers is again reduced to a random killer, attacking whoever he pleases. This is displayed in a pretty outstanding single-take shot in which the killer roams around a Haddonfield neighborhood, walking into people's homes and committing several murders. An interesting detail here is that one of the houses has an infant in it, which Michael looks at and just walks past, showing that he has no interest in killing babies. In order to get him into a one-on-one with Laurie, the writers had to take some drastic measures. They introduce a character named Dr. Sartain, who is Michael's current psychiatrist and is referred to in the movie as the "new Loomis." However, halfway

The 2018 film's Old Man Michael (portrayed here by James Jude Courtney) (*Halloween*, Miramax/Blumhouse, 2018).

through the film, it's revealed that he's insane himself, and is actually responsible for the crash that freed Myers. Later in the film, he transports the detained psychopath to Laurie's house, forcing the confrontation, giving the Shape a reason to attack her and her family.

This one ends with Laurie tricking Michael, trapping him in her death-trap basement, and setting the house on fire. There are several callbacks to the original film, like having Laurie appear behind Michael from a dark hallway and doing a vanishing act after falling off a balcony. She and the family escape while the house burns to the ground, possibly taking him with it once and for all, although it's less of a momentous occasion since he's just a guy that she had encountered once, 40 years ago.

Released in mid–October, just in time for the spooky season, *Halloween* (2018) was an unexpected, massive hit, collecting over $250 million against a cost of somewhere between $10–$15 million, making it the highest-grossing entry in the entire series. It did over $75 million in its opening weekend alone,[11] crushing the numbers of every single entry that came before it. It did more money in its first three days than either of the Zombie entries achieved during their entire runs. It also did something that few of the other sequels did: get good reviews. Its score on the review site, Rotten Tomatoes, sits at 79 percent positive, with most critics praising its atmosphere and the return to classic scares. Normally, a level of success this big would be a clear indicator for a sequel, but this had actually been planned out from the beginning, as the creators had considered shooting two films back to back. Although they didn't go that route, the path to a sequel was clear.

It took a little longer than expected. The next entry, entitled *Halloween Kills*, brought back the entire creative team, and was scheduled to arrive in the fall of 2020, but was delayed, for, uh … obvious reasons. Instead, it was pushed back to the fall of 2021, releasing right before the Halloween season, and featured the same creative team as the 2018 film.

As noted, the team had planned to make two films back to back, so when it was clear that a sequel was going to happen, they laid out their concept for the follow-up. While mapping it all out, they realized that there was enough material to expand the script and go for a trilogy. Given the sensation that the 2018 film had become, Blumhouse was more than pleased with this approach.

Halloween Kills takes place immediately after the last film, picking up with Laurie being taken to the hospital and Michael accidentally rescued by firefighters. Like the first *Halloween II*, the film continues the story of that one night, again taking place on October 31, 2018. We know this conclusively because approximately 37 characters all say that Myers's original attacks were 40 years ago. If you start to have any doubts about how long ago the original film takes place, you will conveniently be reminded of it every five minutes or so in this movie.

Continuity-wise, most everything remains the same here. Michael's mask is burned down the side of it, due to the fire at the house, and the few brief shots of his hands reveal him to still be missing several fingers that Laurie shot off in the last film. There are several nods and changes to the lore of the original film, as we see flashbacks detailing events from later that night. They're clearly different from what we've seen before, as those circumstances have since been erased. Instead, after the incident at the Doyle house, Michael wanders around for a while before ending up back at his own house, where he's captured by police, leading to his incarceration for the next 40 years. There is one slight inconsistency with the last film, as it now seems as if the townspeople are indeed deeply affected by Michael's original rampage.

We're shown several characters that survived the first film, including Marion, again played by Nancy Stephens, returning to her character again after being killed off in *H20*. (She won't make it through this film either.) Tommy Doyle also returns, but obviously a different version than the one that we've met before. He's no longer played by Paul Rudd, and instead the role is filled by Anthony Michael Hall. Lindsay Wallace, the little girl being babysat by Annie Brackett in the original, is on hand as well. She is once again played by Kyle Richards, who had the role back in '78 and then went on to become one of the *Real Housewives of Beverly Hills*. The final returning legacy character is Charles Cyphers as Sheriff Leigh Brackett, father of Annie, who was last seen in the original *Halloween II*. In the original continuity, he had retired and moved to Florida, but here he stayed in Haddonfield and became a security guard for

Kills' burned-up style for Michael's (James Jude Courtney) mask (*Halloween Kills*, Miramax/Blumhouse, 2021).

the hospital. Of this collection of returning characters, the only one to survive the night would be Lindsay Wallace, who narrowly avoids being killed by Myers.

All of the characters, and many of the townsfolk, seem to still be traumatized by the events of 40 years ago, but that doesn't match up to the 2018 film, in which it's stressed that Laurie was alone in her fears. That film puts forth that the Myers killings were just a small footnote in the town's history, and that it was a small tragedy compared to more horrific recent events. Laurie has no one to go to and is treated like an outcast for still fearing Michael, yet this film shows that many of her neighbors shared her worries. It's an odd inconsistency that seems to be a plot point that was devised after the fact, in order to bring back the legacy characters.

Laurie is actually absent for a decent portion of the film, having been taken to the hospital for her injuries, in a sort of mirror of the events of the original *Halloween II*. Her contributions to this entry are fairly minimal, and she doesn't actually encounter Michael in the entire runtime of the film. We get another minor bit of series continuity, as it's revealed that Deputy Hawkins, seemingly killed in the last film, survived his wounds and is also recovering.

Through Hawkins, we get more series lore, as he provides flashbacks to 1978, when it's shown that he was one of the officers responsible for arresting Michael that night, filling in the blanks of what happened at the end of the first movie in this continuity. During these, we get a brief appearance of Loomis, here played by a Donald Pleasence look-alike with some prosthetic assistance.

Another longtime "character" of the series makes a return here, in the form of the Myers house. There's a touch of a continuity error here, as the 2018 film states that the house was torn down after being a target of vandals over the years, but here it's seen intact and renovated. In this film, it's revealed that the house is always where Michael returns after his sprees. It's where they were able to catch him back in 1978, and where he eventually heads in *Kills*. Here, it's currently inhabited by a couple, and for some reason, the police do not station any patrols or units by the house. Considering it's exactly where he went while being hunted the previous time, it's a little unclear why it doesn't cross anyone's mind that he might do so again. As such, the couple just hangs out there until their expected demises. The look of the house is very similar to the original, only with a modernized paint job and finishing, returning it to a styling not seen since *Halloween II*.

The end of *Kills* is clearly intended to set up more entries, as it finishes up on a cliffhanger. After a mob of townsfolk trap Michael and gang up on him, shooting and stabbing him, he is still able to get up and kill what appears to be all of them and then somehow manages to get back to his old house unseen by any of the hundred or so people in the general vicinity. There, he kills Karen, Laurie's daughter, prepping the stage for a final confrontation between him and the Strode family.

The release of this episode was the most unusual in the franchise. Not only did it suffer from the year-long delay, but it was available on the Peacock streaming service on the same date. Like the one before it, this was also a massive success. It premiered to a $49 million weekend, topping the box office, even with people having access to watching it at home. Over the course of its run, it would collect $131 million worldwide, which may have been around half of what the one before did, but still amounted to a huge profit.[12]

At the time of writing this book, the early promotional push for the third entry of this series has begun. It's entitled *Halloween Ends,* releasing in October 2022, again directed by Green. The entire cast from the previous two are returning, promising a true finality to the storyline. It's said to take place four years after the events of *Kills,* and would incorporate elements of the pandemic into the plot. That would place the timeline of the entry in 2022, bringing the series back into real time.

One thing that's for certain is that, even if this new film closes out the story, it will most certainly not be the ending of the *Halloween* franchise. Based on the renewed success, you can either expect them to find a way to continue with this version of things, completely reboot the concept with another remake, or just do as they've done twice before and ignore specific sequels.

It's probably a safe bet that they won't try the whole anthology tactic again, though.

Timeline Summary

Original Timeline

Halloween—October 1978 (date shown on-screen)
Halloween II—October 1978 (picks up immediately after the first, occurring on the same night)
Halloween III: Season of the Witch—October 1982 (extrapolated from days and dates given)
Halloween 4: The Return of Michael Myers—October 1988 (stated to be 10 years after the first two films)

Halloween 5: The Revenge of Michael Myers—October 1989 (stated to be one year after the fourth film)
Halloween 6: The Curse of Michael Myers—October 1995 (stated to be six years after the fifth film)

H20 Timeline

Halloween—October 1978 (date shown on-screen)
Halloween II—October 1978 (picks up immediately after the first, occurring on the same night)
Halloween H20: 20 Years Later—October 1998 (date shown on-screen)
Halloween: Resurrection—October 2001 (said to be three years after *H20*)

RZ Timeline

Rob Zombie's Halloween—2007 (based on year of release)
Rob Zombie's Halloween II—2008 (said to be one year later)

Blumhouse Timeline

Halloween—October 1978 (date shown on-screen)
Halloween 2018—October 2018 (said to be 40 years after the original)
Halloween Kills—October 2018 (picks up immediately after the last one, occurring on the same night)
Halloween Ends—October 2022 (timeframe given in advance press)

CHAPTER 3

Child's Play

After discussing series with completely fractured timelines, it's nice to talk about one that lines up a little more clearly. Of the major horror franchises, the *Child's Play* movies are the most coherent. Although they're not often considered of the same caliber as their peers, the *Chucky* movies actually hold up as not only being more consistently entertaining, but also having a stronger sense of continuity. Even if they don't exactly understand how dates work.

The series began back in 1988 with *Child's Play*, directed by horror legend Tom Holland, who also cowrote the story from a script by Don Mancini. The original script was entitled *Batteries Not Included*, but it was soon apparent that it would need to be changed, due to the Steven Spielberg–produced family-friendly film with the same name. It was briefly switched to *Blood Buddy*, before finally settling on the title that we would all come to know and love.

It starts off with introducing us to the main focus of the series, serial killer Charles Lee Ray, played brilliantly by Brad Dourif. He's shot and killed by police, but not before conducting a voodoo spell to transfer his soul into a doll. We also meet Andy Barclay and his mother, and it's Andy's birthday, so he gets the gift he's most excited for: a Good Guy doll. But not just any Good Guy doll. Chucky. After revealing his true identity, it's discovered that the only way to get out of the doll's body would be to transfer his soul into the person he first revealed his identity to, which would be Andy.

In terms of establishing a timeline, the first film actually manages to avoid giving us a set date, but it does contain several clues. The toy store has Christmas decorations up, yet no one seems to mention the holiday, which means it's early on in the season, possibly early November or so. There are also a few mentions of Andy's age, placing him at six years old, and we see that it's his birthday, so he's newly six.

The look of Chucky is firmly established in this movie as well. When he's in normal doll mode, the Good Guy is heavily influenced by the My Buddy dolls from the same time period. The face is innocent and cherubic, with tiny overalls and sneakers. His hair is wild red tufts, and his face changes when Charles reveals his true self, becoming more angular and contorted.

The film also introduces the concept that Chucky only has a few days to make the transfer, as his soul is fusing with the doll body. If he remains there for too long, he will be trapped, and the toy starts becoming more and more human as the time runs out. This is shown through the movie by altering the doll puppet as the film goes on. Its details become more prominent, and his hairline even starts to recede to match that of his living persona.

The rules are pretty clearly laid out in an exposition scene with Ray's voodoo mentor, who explains the situation to him. The amount of time he has is never discussed, but we see the process play out over just a few days. The specifics of the ritual are also on display. The spell caster just takes their subject and lays hands on it, whether it be a doll or a child, and starts the Damballa Chant, which consists of the words, "Ade due Damballa. Give me the power, I beg of you!" After reciting the words, massive storm clouds will appear in the sky, raining down lightning to accompany the spell.

The film also sees Chucky seeking revenge on the police officer who shot him in the beginning, played by Chris Sarandon. He had previously worked with Holland on *Fright Night*, in which he played the villain, Jerry Dandridge, but he takes on the hero role here. Considering that Sarandon's two most prominent roles, Dandridge and *Princess Bride*'s Prince Humperdinck, are despicable characters, it's nice to see him as

Chucky's classic original look (*Child's Play*, MGM, 1988).

more of a good guy. In the finale, the final showdown between the doll and the family leads to our villain being set on fire, having his limbs shot off, decapitated, and finally shot in the heart, which seems to kill him.

The budget of the film was actually pretty healthy, at $9 million. Comparatively, the same year saw the release of *Friday the 13th Part VII* and *Halloween 4*, and the combined costs of both of those films would only amount to around $8 million, so MGM, the studio that released it, was taking a bit of a risk. They compounded this by skipping the October release to put the film out in early November, usually not a strong time for horror films. This didn't seem to hinder things, since it debuted at number 1, besting the holiday film, *Ernest Saves Christmas*, and the action sequel, *Iron Eagle II*. After a $6.5 million opening weekend, it would go on to bring in a total of $43 million worldwide,[1] cementing it as a certified hit for the studio.

With numbers like that, sequel didn't take long, and *Child's Play 2* was released two years later, in 1990. Tom Holland didn't return to the director's chair, and was instead replaced with John Lafia, one of the writers of the first film. It also switched studios, with Universal purchasing the rights to the series to continue with it. MGM/UA would retain the rights to the first film, which would make for some interesting issues a little further down the road. UA chose to sell off the rights since they were going through an ownership change, and the new regime had decided that they would no longer be in the business of making horror films.

Child's Play 2 begins with the toy company that makes Good Guy dolls taking the remains of the Chucky doll and restoring it, in an effort to disprove the Barclay family's story. Andy's mother is deemed to be mentally unstable and placed under psychiatric care, while Andy himself is placed in the foster system, ending up in the care of a new family. Of course, the restored doll comes back to life, and Chucky is back, still committed to transferring his soul into Andy.

The logic of the spell has pretty much gone out the window at this point, since the initial ruling was that his heart had to be destroyed, which it was, and the doll was mostly human at that point. When restoring the doll, they should have been confronted with mostly organic remains, considering how much blood Chucky bled out in the last film, but it's possible that it reverted to an inanimate state after death, because magic. After reviving the doll, possibly through an electric current in the opening scene, the spell is seemingly reset, and Charles once again has a few days before becoming a living stuffed animal.

The rules are basically the same here, and the action is essentially

Perhaps the most famous Chucky shot (*Child's Play 2*, Universal, 1990).

a repeat of that of the first film. Chucky has to locate Andy and do the Damballa before becoming human, and he infiltrates the new family to do so. Of course, again, no one believes Andy when bad things start to happen and people start dying off.

There wasn't much in the way of returning characters, with only Chucky and Andy returning to the action. Dourif would return to voice the evil doll, while Alex Vincent would again portray the young victim. Originally, Catherine Hicks and Chris Sarandon were intended to reprise their roles as Karen and Mike, appearing in a courtroom scene at the onset of the film. However, in order to help reduce the film's budget, this scene was eventually cut, and the consequences of it are just stated.

Instead, Andy is taken in by a new family, played by *American Werewolf in London*'s Jenny Agutter and Bud the C.H.U.D., Gerrit Graham We're also introduced to the character of Kyle, another foster child placed with the same family as Andy, who ends up helping him out during the film's finale.

There is a certain amount of hand-waving required in the setup of the film in order to facilitate having Andy in the foster home. It has to be assumed that Mike and his partner both stated for the record that the doll was not possessed by the spirit of Charles Lee Ray, and that Karen was alone in her defense of Andy. It's insinuated that they did so in order to protect their careers, although it seems a little bit suspect that Mike would do this. His character was shown to be fairly altruistic and helpful, and it slightly stains his image to know that he was okay with protecting himself while Andy's mother would end up losing custody of her child and being locked away.

As far as the timeline goes, it's clear that some time has passed between the two films, although they never truly clarify exactly how much. It's presumed that the same two years that elapsed in real time have done so in the film universe. The only date that appears in the movie is on a police report about Andy, which gives his birth date as either January or February of 1983. Since we know that he was six years old in the first movie, and it was at the time of his birthday, it would seem like the most likely year for that one would actually be early 1989, and since the department store in the opening of *Part 1* had Christmas stuff up, it seems like January would be the more likely option.

The climactic fight of the film takes place in a Good Guy doll factory, in which dozens of dolls are being manufactured and boxed, in what is generally considered to be the best finale of the series. In it, we get the revelation that Charles has actually been in the plastic body for too long, and it's no longer possible for him to transfer his soul, trapping him in that state. In the battle that follows, Chucky's hand is torn off, which he replaces with a knife, and he's placed in some sort of crushing machine that completely mangles him, leaving him without a bottom half, melted down by hot plastic, and finally having his entire head blown up, leaving very little trace of him left.

With a modest budget boost to $13 million, the film would open strong with a $10.7 million weekend, again hitting the top spot. When all was said and done, the sequel raked in $35 million worldwide,[2] which represented a slight drop for the first film, but was enough to ensure that the series would continue.

In fact, the script for the third film had already been completed. The producers had had Mancini prepare the script ahead of the second's release, with the intentions of greenlighting it upon its success. Since that film did well, they moved forward with it, giving a very tight deadline of releasing the next entry nine months later.

And so, in 1991, *Child's Play 3* was released, with TV director Jack Bender taking the chair. Mancini's original concept for the film involved melting the remains of the Chucky doll into a batch of plastic that the toy company would then use to make multiple dolls, each with the soul of Chucky in it, an idea which was dropped due to budgetary reasons, but one which the writer would return to about five films later.

Instead, while the melted plastic notion is indeed still used, it only produces one killer doll, who once again begins his pursuit of Andy Barclay. However, in the early part of the film, several representatives from the toy company state that it's been eight years since the little boy brought them the bad press of saying his doll killed people, and they also state that he's now 16 years old. That means that there's actual a big time jump between the second film and this one, and would also place him at eight years old during that film's time frame. Because of that, we now know that there's a two-year gap in between the first and second films and 2 would actually take place in 1991. Since this film is eight years after that, 3 would then occur in 1999, a full eight years ahead of its time of release.

Andy is back, but recast, since the age difference would be too apparent with original actor Alex Vincent, so Justin Whalin would take over the role. He's now in military school, after a string of foster homes, and has a reputation for being rebellious. At the school, we meet a new cast of characters including young Tyler, an eight-year-old cadet. Kirsty's dad from *Hellraiser* (Andrew Robinson) is also here as a sadistic barber who has an obsession with shaving people's heads.

With a new actor playing Andy, that makes Dourif the sole remaining cast member, as he once again steps behind the microphone to lend Chucky his unmistakable voice.

After Chucky is revived, he makes his way to the academy and reveals himself to Tyler, giving Charles Lee Ray a new host to try to inhabit. Again, for one reason or another, resurrecting his doll form resets the spell and his time frame, so he once again has a few days in which to finish the soul transference spell. This is a new addition to the background of the spell, although it doesn't particularly contradict elements that had come before, merely adjusts them for a new situation.

In terms of continuity, the time jump covers a lot of the dirty work there, since the only real link to the prior entries is the presence of Andy, and the dates they talk about do make sense. The biggest problem here is that the extreme length of the time jump places them farther in the future than the film's release date. Normally, this would cause issues with hair styles, clothing, and possibly car models, but the military school setting assists with that. Since the uniforms and hairstyle are standard issue, they skirt around any fashion inconsistencies.

Also, Chucky's appearance remains the same, with the only modifications being some superficial ones with the improved doll models they used. The biggest innovation here was the addition of computer software to assist with Chucky's dialogue, which made the animatronic doll's lip movements more closely match Dourif's recorded dialogue, creating a more realistic look.

Following a number of violent interactions, Chucky's final attempt to place his soul into Tyler takes them to a conveniently located carnival, and into a dark ride attraction. There, an errant prop slices off half of the doll's face, and he once again loses an arm before falling into a giant fan that chops him up into pieces.

Chucky does his take on Two-Face (with Jeremy Sylvers) (*Child's Play 3*, Universal, 1991).

Unfortunately, the film didn't quite live up to its predecessors at the theaters, pulling in a modest $20 million worldwide, a sharp drop from the second film's numbers.[3] Although the budget was still the same $13 million as that one, and it still amounted to a profit at the box office, it seemed as if the series' popularity was waning. The film was dealt a further insult when it was used in a court case concerning the murder of James Bulger, a two-year-old boy in England. His killers were two 10-year-old boys and there were allegations that they were inspired to recreate one of the scenes that they had seen in the film. Although most of the claims were eventually dismissed as unfounded, the controversy followed the film, staining its reputation, or as much of a reputation as the third entry of *Child's Play* movies can have.

Because of the scandal—although let's be honest, mostly due to the poor box office of the third entry—the series went away for a little while and didn't resurface for another seven years. Then, in 1998, it became time to reinvigorate the franchise, with Don Mancini and producer David Kirschner realizing that they would need to shake up the formula a bit. What with *Scream* in the theaters, redefining horror films, they decided to move forward with *Bride of Chucky*.

It was a new take on the character, and eliminated Andy Barclay from the storyline. Mancini had been inspired by *Bride of Frankenstein*, and thought to introduce a new foil for the killer in Tiffany, a female counterpart, played by Jennifer Tilly. Her character is retroactively added into the tale of Charles Lee Ray, establishing her as his girlfriend in the time before his death.

They tapped Ronny Yu to direct, who was then an unknown commodity in the American market, although he had proven himself overseas. He would later go on to make *Freddy vs. Jason*, and then just kind of vanish from the horror world.

The elimination of Andy from the story once again left Chucky as the only returning character, and Dourif as the sole recurring cast member. It would also add a then mostly unknown Katherine Heigl to the cast, as well as Jack Tripper (John Ritter) and the late Alexis Arquette.

The story picks up where *3* left off, with Chucky still in pieces from being chopped up in that fan, as his former lover, Tiffany, recovers his corpse from a police evidence locker. There are several in-jokes here, as those lockers also seem to contain references to other franchises, with appearances of Jason's hockey mask, Freddy's glove, Leatherface's chainsaw, and Michael Myers's mask. There's a lot of discussion in the community as to whether or not that this proves that the *Chucky* films are set in the same universe as all of the others, and I suppose it's possible, although that's clearly not a mask that Jason would ever have worn. And come on, it's a chainsaw. That could belong to anybody.

After stitching Chucky back together, Tiffany revives him with another voodoo spell, which apparently once again resets the timer for him, giving him another few days to implant himself into another body. This time, he kills Tiffany and puts her soul into a female doll, which doesn't really appear to be a Good Guy doll, just a model that looks similar. The two team up to cause chaos and to place their souls into a pair of humans in order to renew their unhealthy love affair and continue their killing spree.

As far as the timeline goes, there's a lot to go with here, although it does disrupt what we already know. Early on in the film, we're shown newspaper clippings about the death of Charles Lee Ray, and it places that event as occurring on November 9, 1988, a little earlier than we had already determined, but since that date is repeated later, on Charles's tombstone, it's pretty clear that it's the correct one. If that's the case, then the first movie is 1988, with the second film taking place in 1990, and the third occurring eight years later, in 1998. The only issue this causes is the police report with Andy's date of birth, since the date given would only make him five in the first film, but it's pretty possible that it's just an error on the report. Meanwhile, in this film, Tiffany states that Chucky died and she's been searching for him for 10 years, giving us a time frame for this one and placing it in 1998. This is backed up by a shot of vehicles registration stickers that state it's '98, so it seems as if this entry happens a short time after the third one, and Chucky has been freshly chopped up.

In terms of continuity, there's some confusion, as it introduces the concept of the Heart of Damballa, a magical amulet that will allow them to switch into whatever bodies that they want. It's a bit of an odd addition since it would have been extremely advantageous for Chucky to have had it before this, and seems like something he would have sought out earlier. There is a way to justify this from within the film, though. This entry makes a joke out of the fact that Tiffany uses a book to revive Charles, and it's a part of the popular "Dummies" series entitled "Voodoo for Dummies." Theoretically, in this world, there's a mass-market book that has a spell in it that can straight up allow you to transfer your soul into things. Based on what we saw in the first film, it's just a matter of knowing the words to do it, so that would seem to be pretty irresponsible for a book company to just publish all willy-nilly. Anyway, in this book, there's a picture of the Heart of Damballa and a description of what it does. It's very possible that Chucky was completely unaware of what the medallion was capable of until reading this passage in the book, assuming it to just be a cool necklace before.

The overall look of Chucky changed entirely with this entry, further distancing it from its predecessors. After being stitched up by Tiffany, he takes on a FrankenChucky look, to go with the whole "Bride of" theme. His face features several large metal fasteners to hold it together, and his hair is patchier and wilder than before. Any semblance of him blending in to look like a regular doll is more or less gone here.

The storyline here involves Chucky and Tiffany trying to travel to New Jersey to reclaim the Heart, hitching a ride with a pair of eloping

Introducing the now-iconic Franken-Chucky (*Bride of Chucky*, Universal, 1998).

young lovers. Along the way, the human couple end up getting blamed for the killings, and tensions arise between the two as they begin to suspect each other, instead of the weird dolls in the back of their van.

Of course, the ending of the film features a final battle, with Tiffany betraying Charles and ending up stabbed because of it. She's stabbed in the heart, bringing that plot element back into play, seemingly killing her. Finally, while standing in his own grave, Chucky is shot through the heart again, but not before proclaiming that he will be back ... because he always comes back.

The film would actually end with a setup for further action, with the revelation that Tiffany was actually pregnant, as an evil baby doll erupts from her body to attack an investigating police officer. She's pregnant because she and Chucky had sex earlier. I think I forgot to mention that the dolls had sex as their bodies were becoming more human. I feel like that's the type of thing I usually would have mentioned.

The film came with a higher price tag, being budgeted at $25 million, the most expensive of the entire franchise, and represented a bit of risk. Once again, that paid off, as it debuted to a strong $11.8 million weekend, the highest of the franchise so far. In its total run, it would make over $50 million worldwide,[4] and remains the highest-grossing entry in the series.

The new take on the characters would be met a good deal of appreciation from the fan base, as well as bringing a whole new generation into the fold. Although reviews were still very critical, as they generally are for horror films, they were on the whole more favorable than the previous few. It's often viewed as one of the best of the franchise, with Brad Dourif choosing it as his personal favorite.

Because of the success, preproduction began on the next episode almost immediately. Mere days after *Bride* debuted to big numbers, Mancini began work on a script. Unfortunately, a series of issues caused it to be put on the shelf. First off, Ronny Yu was unable to return for the follow-up due to scheduling issues, and then Universal balked at the screenplay, deciding that it was too comedy-based. It also contained the note that it was "too gay," a criticism I'm sure the openly gay Mancini truly appreciated.

Eventually, six years later, it made it to the screen with 2004's *Seed of Chucky*, although only approved with a much smaller $12 million budget, one of the lowest of the series. Mancini himself moved into the director's chair, taking control of his franchise for the first time.

The story picks up where the last one left off, as Tiffany gives birth to her demonic offspring. We're introduced to that child, who is being held in a circus sideshow as part of a fake ventriloquist act. The owner

Chucky and Tiffany return to life (*Seed of Chucky*, Rogue/Relativity, 2004).

tells the crowd that he found the doll in a cemetery six years ago, placing us in 2004 and keeping the series in real time. After escaping, the child finds his parents, whose doll bodies are actually being used as props in a film version of their story.

Here's where the "too gay" comments came from, as it's revealed that the child is confused about his gender, not really fitting in with either role. As such, they name him either Glen or Glenda, in a reference to the Ed Wood film of the same name, and proceed to help him determine his sexual identity. Since Mancini himself was gay, he wanted to use the film to explore LGBTQ+ themes, much to the chagrin of Universal.

The continuity remains mostly consistent, with the Heart of Damballa once again featuring into the action, and the looks of the characters remaining the same as their previous incarnation. Both actors would return to their doll roles, although they would be the only returning cast members, as Jade and Jesse from the last one would not be mentioned.

It does introduce an unusual meta twist with the addition of Tilly and several other real-life celebrities appearing as exaggerated versions of themselves. Special effects artists Tony Gardner appears and is killed on-screen, rapper Redman is gutted by Tiffany, and John Waters plays a paparazzi who is killed by acid dumped on his head.

At this point, the details of the voodoo spell that kicks everything off have been pretty much put aside. The concept of the doll bodies becoming more and more human is barely mentioned, and the idea that Chucky can be killed by destroying his heart has been definitively shelved. Instead, it's become apparent that as long as the Heart is involved, Chucky can constantly be revived, provided that he has a vessel to inhabit. Since the film company decided to use the actual bodies of Chucky and Tiffany, their souls are still dormant within, regardless of heart damage. I'm not entirely sure of the logistics or legal ramifications of using the actual dolls as movie props, and how that would even benefit the special effects department. Seems like that would actually make their job more difficult in the long run. Plus, I'm not really convinced that it would be a selling point for the film, since "oh, hey, the dolls in our movie are the actual killer dolls that went on a rampage a few years ago" doesn't really sound like the sort of thing that studios would want to promote.

In the conclusion, a number of rapid-fire events occur, leading to Chucky choosing to remain a doll, Tiffany switching into Jennifer Tilly's body, and Glen killing his dad with a few well-placed axe blows, then separating his male and female identities into twin children. The coda of the film actually jumps ahead five years, with that one scene taking place in 2009, with the twins at five years old. And, yeah, it's a lot, but the whole tone of the film is a lot. It's very over the top and veers far more into the absurd humor of *Bride*, becoming a horror comedy instead of the straightforward slasher origins of the series.

Like Universal, audiences also rejected this idea, with most considering it to be the worst in the series. In its theatrical run, it only pulled in $25 million worldwide, debuting at number 4 and doing $8.8 million in its first weekend.[5] Considering that they pulled back the budget so drastically, it was still quite profitable, but it was a big step down from the previous film, and was considered a box office failure.

As *Seed* proved to be lackluster both at the ticket booth and in its audience reaction, the franchise went away for a while. It's longest hiatus to date, actually, as it took a full nine years for any further installments. It wasn't until 2013's *Curse of Chucky* that the killer doll returned, again directed by Don Mancini. It was actually the first in the series to skip the theaters and go straight to video, and was produced on a tiny budget of $2.8 million, a 10th of the budget of *Bride of Chucky.*

Before release, *Curse* was promoted as a reboot of the series, returning it to its classic horror roots and stepping away from the comedy elements of the last two entries. Both Don Mancini and producer David Kirschner would give interviews stating that the film would be a darker and grittier remake, going back to the feel of the original.

It focused on a new character, Nica, played by Brad Dourif's real-life daughter, Fiona, and her family, who receive a Chucky doll in the mail one day. It's a brand-new Good Guy, similar to the appearance of the one from the first movie. Without fail, a series of unexplained accidents start to occur and the bodies begin to pile up, hinting that the doll is not what it appears to be. But then, they pull a fast one, since about two-thirds of the way into the movie it's revealed to be a continuation of the original timeline. The Chucky doll has some prosthetics covering up the stitches in his face, allowing him to appear like a regular doll.

There's also a sequence in which Nica researches Charles Lee Ray, finding several newspaper articles about him, and they show a date of December 27, 1988, which again confirms the first film as taking place in '88, but does confuse the date. Previously, we had been shown his shooting taking place in early November, not December.

That's not the only continuity confusion, since this one really plays around with the rules of Chucky's mortality. In the past, the longer his soul stayed in the doll, the more human it became, and wounds would end up manifesting in real blood. In this one, however, there are several instances that contradict this. At one point, Chucky's entire head is removed, with no effect, and he's easily able to pop it back on. His head had been removed previously, in the first film, and he was still able to function, but it was a much bloodier and messier affair. Similarly, while in close combat, Nica manages to stab the doll in the chest with a large knife, and the only thing that appears from the wound is stuffing. Earlier, we would have seen blood coming from the wound, so it's possible that this is still early enough in the process that he hasn't started

The covered-up and renewed look (*Curse of Chucky*, Universal, 2013).

becoming human yet, or has found access to a spell to prolong those effects. There was at least a handful of years between the last film and this one, and there's apparently a whole book full of voodoo spells for him to work with, so it should be expected that he would learn some new tricks.

Another slight variation with Chucky himself, although merely a behind-the-scenes one, is the technology used in bringing him to life. This film features the very first instance of using a fully CGI version of the character, showing him walking down a flight of stairs. It's not terrible, but it is slightly jarring, and a moment that fans point to as a flaw.

Our timeline comes into play a little later, as Chucky reveals himself to Nica, explaining his hidden past with her family. It seems he was obsessed with her mother, stalking her, and in fact, on the night that police shot him, they were coming from his assault on her mother, which is a slight variation from what we had been told before. In *Bride of Chucky*, Tiffany says that she was with Charles the night before he died, although it's possible that she was only referring to earlier in the evening, before he went to the Pierces' household. While telling this story to Nica, Chucky states that he's been looking for her for 25 years, which would place this one in 2013, about four years after the epilogue of *Seed*.

During these flashback scenes to the night he died, we get our first appearances of Brad Dourif playing the human version of Charles since the very first film. His age difference is slightly obvious, although merely a minor detail.

The final fight results in Nica's entire family dead at the hands of the Good Guy, and the police blaming her for the crimes, and taking Chucky in as evidence. We're treated to a repeat of the sequence from the opening of *Bride*, with Tiffany reappearing to collect her man, and a post-credits scene locks the continuity down even further. There, we jump ahead six months and see the return of Andy Barclay, once again played by Alex Vincent. He says that it's his birthday tomorrow, so we'd be set later on in 2013 then, and depending on which newspaper has the correct date of Lee Ray's death, it would be either November or December. He receives a mysterious package, much like Nica in the beginning of the film, which contains Chucky, but Andy is prepared and shoots him directly in the face.

As a very minor detail, Andy is on the phone with his mother, showing that somewhere along the way, their relationship was restored, and she was released from whatever care she was under. He also mentions for her to say hello to Mike, which is probably a reference to Officer Mike Norris. If so, it states the Karen and Mike have reconnected, and can be interpreted as them being in some sort of relationship together.

With a much smaller budget, the stakes were much lower, and the film received mainly positive reactions from critics and fans alike. Since it didn't play in theaters, there aren't any box office numbers to compare to the earlier entries, but it was fairly successful in DVD sales, and a follow-up became imminent. Mancini confirmed that he was working on a new installment immediately after *Curse*'s release, although it took four more years for *Cult of Chucky* to debut.

It was another direct-to-video release, and more than doubled the budget of *Curse*, coming in at a $7 million price tag, and by this point, it was just expected that Mancini would be handling both scripting and directing duties. Not only did Brad Dourif return as the voice of Chucky, but we'd also see Fiona Dourif return as Nica, and the film would feature several returning actors from the franchise.

Cult opens after the finale of *Curse*, showing us Andy, still dealing with the ghosts of his past, and gives some nods to the prior films with pictures of Andy's mother and Kyle from the second film. It also shows that he still has the remains of the Chucky head from the last one's epilogue, and it's still alive and talking.

The credits introduce several elements of our timeline, placing the events of *Curse* in early January, which is a bit confusing, since the post credit scene takes place six months after the bulk of the main film. So if that was in January, the final moment occurs in July or so of 2013, although Andy states that his birthday is tomorrow. Unfortunately, the first film also featured the character's birthday, and it was around the time of Charles Lee Ray's shooting, which, according to the previous film, was in December. Or November. Whichever. It just wasn't July.

The dates in the credits also show a report on Nica, which gives her birth date as 1987. This is also an issue, since the last film showed her still in her mother's belly on the night Ray died, which was shown to be in 1988, one year after this given birth year. This could likely be attributed to a minor clerical error, similar to the issue with Andy's birthdate earlier in the series.

Regardless of these minor errors, we're shown that Nica has been institutionalized after the murder of her family, and her doctor says that occurred four years ago, placing *Cult* firmly in 2017, and keeping the series in real time.

The biggest element that is brought into this film is the concept of having multiple dolls. It seems that in the interim between the films, Chucky has been doing more research into the voodoo spells that gave him life, and he has discovered a new chant that would allow him to multiply his soul into extra vessels. We're introduced to five of them over the course of this film. The first is the remains of the head in Andy's apartment, but there is also another doll present at the institution, containing the killer soul. When another Good Guy doll is brought into a therapy session for Nica to face, Chucky duplicates his soul into that form as well, making two of them running around the hospital. And then, when Andy ships yet another one there, this one with a military buzz cut, it is animated as well. Finally, Chucky places his soul into Nica's body, superseding her personality and taking it over, becoming human again for the first time in the series. As mentioned earlier, this was a plot point that Mancini had intended to use in *Child's Play 3*, but couldn't, and it's brought back into the series here.

Along with both Andy and Nica returning, this one also features a few other characters, including Jennifer Tilly as Tiffany in Jennifer Tilly's body, as well as a duplicate of herself in yet another Tiffany doll, presumably using the soul multiplication spell. Also, in a post-credits tease, the character of Kyle returns momentarily, called into action by Andy. She is once again played by Christine Elise, returning to the role after 27 years.

The movie actually ends in a cliffhanger, with Chucky winning for the first time in the franchise. He is able to transfer his soul into Nica's body, taking it over and reuniting with Tiffany to drive off together. Andy is left trapped in the asylum, locked in one of the rooms. The open ending was intentional, as Mancini was actively developing a TV series and intended the loose ends in the film to be picked up in the show. But before that could happen, something even weirder would have to happen.

Multiple Chucky dolls wreak havoc (*Cult of Chucky,* Universal, 2017).

You see, although the rights to the characters would bounce around from company to company, MGM still owned the original 1988 film. They announced their plans to produce a remake. It would be a completely separate entity from what was currently being done, and would actually exist side by side, a possible first for the horror industry: a remake of a property while the original property is still ongoing. Rights snafus like this had occurred previously, like the James Bond anomaly *Never Say Never Again*, but horror fans had not yet seen its like.

So in 2019, MGM released *Child's Play*, directed by Lars Klevberg, which used the framing of the first film, but updated and altered it. It still focuses on Andy Barclay and his mother, with him receiving a doll that comes to life and begins killing, and still has police Detective Norris on the case, but it eliminates practically everything else.

Instead of a Good Guy doll, we're introduced to Buddi, a Wi-Fi integrated smart toy. Its appearance is vaguely similar to the original design, but modernized and made to look less like a cuddly kid's toy. Its face is more angular, lacking the Cabbage Patch feel of the original— and frankly, looking a little more disturbing than one would expect for a mass market toy. The voodoo element, as well as the serial killer aspect, are totally erased, instead going in the direction of a corrupt AI, without the necessary safety protocols to keep it from becoming a psychopath. Before this film, the importance of safety protocols in children's toys was never really discussed, but the remake brought forward the realization of just how close toys can be to murderous automatons, with just one alteration of code.

Being a remake, it required an entirely new cast, without even any meta cameos from the original actors. With Brad Dourif not taking part of the entry, Mark Hamill took over the voice, bringing a different

The creepy Buddi doll look from the remake (*Child's Play*, United Artists, 2019).

and less maniacal take to the character. His Buddi was more inquisitive and had a certain innocence to it, based upon the notion of the doll not understanding exactly what was wrong with what it was doing. April Ludgate would step into the role of Andy's mom, while child actor Gabriel Bateman would become the new Andy. Mike Norris would also factor into the new storyline, now played by Brian Tyree Henry.

Another of the big changes is the aging of Andy from six to 13, which allows the character to fight back more, but does raise the question of why a teenager would want to carry around a Buddi. It can be reasoned that the whole "smart toy" aspect would make it more desirable to a 13-year-old, but it still looks like a My Buddy doll, so I'm not really buying it.

Seemingly set in modern times, the film confirms its setting with the gym membership card of one of Chucky's victims, which is dated 2018. The time period is rather interesting, since a flash of a phone's screen places the film in October, and yet there's an entire sequence in which a character is removing Christmas lights. Also, that same character is then killed in the middle of his watermelon patch, which is full of them, ready to pick. With the film being set in Chicago in October, and considering that watermelons are in season in the earlier part of the summer, the actual time frame is a little perplexing.

Although the intention was to make the scenarios more realistic by subtracting the supernatural and voodoo elements from the script, the film instead replaces them with the even more unbelievable Wi-Fi aspects. In this version, Chucky is produced by a company called Kaslan, which makes a series of interconnected products. The Buddi dolls are intended to be able to link up to them and interact with things like your television or fridge. Somehow, this equates to Chucky just being able to hack into any Kaslan product and completely control it, without a password or access. He's even able to control a seatbelt. That appears just be a regular seatbelt.

In the film's main storyline, Chucky becomes obsessed with being Andy's friend, but has a hard time learning what friends actually want, which obviously leads to murder. By the end, the doll has kidnapped Andy's mother, leading to a face-off that sees the Buddi getting shot, stabbed, decapitated, and then burned in a barrel.

Although the film ends with a setup for more entries, with another Buddi doll's eyes lighting up, signifying that the AI code was able to transfer into another unit, any follow-ups were dependent on the box office success. And it was a success, bringing in a worldwide haul of around $45 million against a budget of $10 million,[6] with both critical and audience responses being generally positive. Despite all that, there still hasn't been any word on a sequel, with Klevberg stating that they were still awaiting approval from MGM.

Meanwhile, the original continuity continues, making *Child's Play* one of the few long-running horror franchises that are still set within their original continuities. In 2021, Mancini finally realized his vision of a TV show, as Syfy launched *Chucky*, an ongoing series focusing on the further exploits of the doll.

The first season ran for eight episodes and was overseen by Mancini, who would also cowrite several episodes, as well as directing the premiere. It would also feature a number of returning cast members from the films, as well as establishing several new ones.

At first, it seems completely independent of the movies, detailing a group of high school students in Hackensack, New Jersey, Chucky's home town. New character Jake buys a Good Guy doll from a yard sale for use in an art project, and I'm pretty sure that you can figure out what comes next. Along the way, there are a number of deaths and revelations, as various aspects of the killer's past are uncovered through flashbacks.

Several episodes in, we start to see some of the elements from the films being merged into the new stories through the addition of the legacy characters. Andy is back, reunited with Kyle, on the hunt for the last remaining Chucky dolls. We also catch up with Tiffany and Nica, who is still being controlled by the soul of Charles. Their roles feature the return of all the original actors, and include Fiona Dourif taking on the extra duty of playing a younger version of Charles in flashbacks. This is achieved through a healthy dose of makeup and prosthetics, and is a little jarring and contradictory to his appearance in *Cult*.

The flashbacks actually establish quite a bit of Chucky's life before becoming a doll, and cement quite a bit of continuity. We're shown all the way back to 1965, with a young Charles at seven years old, placing his date of birth in 1958. That would make him 30 years old when his body died. There's also a sequence in 1972, with him at 14 years old, meeting up with a young Eddie Caputo, his accomplice in the first film. More flashbacks would see him in the '80s depicting him meeting Tiffany for the first time and their whirlwind romance, along with him discovering voodoo for the first time. The final one shows the night that Charles is shot, in 1988, with him and Tiff having a big fight and her being the one who gave the tip to Officer Norris on where to find him.

There is a pretty massive timeline error involving the series, creating some controversy about when it is supposed to be set. When Chucky kills Jake's father, his tombstone is shown, giving his date of death as

October 2021. This would make it seem as if four years had passed between *Cult of Chucky* and the TV show, again keeping the franchise in real time. However, later in the show, when Nica is able to regain control of her body, she is informed that it's November 8. She is shocked by this, stating that it's been two weeks since her body was taken over. This is a big issue, since it would place *Cult* in *2021*, which would contradict several things that were stated in that film. It's possible that the show takes place a little later in 2017, but that tombstone would seem to dispute that, as well as several songs being listened to having been released after that date. Although Mancini himself seems to back up the "several weeks" comment online, it's more logical to assume that it is indeed four years later, and the series is set in 2021. The man who tells Nica the date omits the year, only giving the day and date, which could prompt her to make the assumption of two weeks, unaware that she's actually been out of control for several years instead.

The finale ends with multiple cliffhangers, leaving several characters' fates up in the air. After Chucky is able to obtain a small army of Good Guy dolls, he prepares to ship them all over the country and sets off an explosion that seemingly kills Andy and Kyle. In the very end, Andy is revealed to be alive, and he manages to hijack the shipment of Chucky dolls, but is then held at gunpoint by a Tiffany doll. It's unclear if Kyle also survived the explosion. Nica is also given a grim ending, since the human Tiffany, still in the body of Jennifer Tilly, has amputated her arms and legs to prevent her from getting away from her. The three lead cast members all survive, but Chucky is revealed to still be around, setting up the next season.

Season 2 has already been greenlit, and shooting has begun. It is expected to be released in the fall of 2022 and will feature the return of the entire core cast, including Devon Sawa. He played dual roles as twin brothers in the first season, and both were killed, so his role remains a mystery.

Timeline Summary

Child's Play—December 1988 (based on the gravestone from *Bride of Chucky*)

Child's Play 2—1990 (two years later based on Andy's age given as eight, instead of six as in the first film)

Child's Play 3—1998 (said to be eight years after the events of *2*)

Bride of Chucky—later in 1998 (based on Tiffany saying she's been searching 10 years)

Seed of Chucky—2004 (based on the carnival barker saying he found
　　Glen six years ago)
Curse of Chucky—January 2013 (based on Chucky saying he's been
　　waiting 25 years)
Cult of Chucky—winter 2017 (based on news clippings shown)
Chucky TV show—October 2021 (based on Lucas's gravestone)

Remake Timeline

Child's Play–October 2018 (based on the membership card showing
　　2018)

CHAPTER 4

A Nightmare on Elm Street

It's easy to forget just exactly how big Freddy Krueger was. At one point, the character was as much a part of the public zeitgeist as Mickey Mouse. He was everywhere. On the big screen, on the small screen, on your stereo, in books, and hell, he even had his own 900 number. So, with the series being as popular as it was, with as many eyes on it as there were, was there a dedication to its making sense?

The dream began back in 1984 with the original *A Nightmare on Elm Street*, written and directed by Wes Craven. Although he had already made an impact on the horror world with *Last House on the Left*, *The Hills Have Eyes*, and, uh…. *Swamp Thing*, this would mark his most high-profile project to date.

The storyline sets up all the elements that will shape the franchise. A group of high school students keep seeing a mysterious man in their dreams who is trying to kill them. They all have the same visions, and it turns out that when he harms you in the dream, that same injury will translate to the waking world, and the group starts getting killed off. The perpetrator is of course Freddy Krueger, who was apparently killed years ago. It seems that he murdered a bunch of children in the area and was caught, but was let off on a technicality. The parents of the town banded together to get their vengeance, burning him alive. Now he's after their children again, this time using their nap times to do it.

The look of Freddy is established, debuting his trademark Christmas sweater, with the red and green horizontal stripes, and his dusty fedora. His skin is burned, and his weapon of choice is a single glove with razors attached to the ends, like finger knives. In the dreams, he does start to show some reality-warping abilities, like creating images of dead friends, and making holes in some stairs to hinder going up them, but they seem somewhat limited at this point. He also proves to be impervious to harm here, able to chop off his own fingers and then make them instantly reappear, as well as pulling off his entire face.

The basic rules of what happens when Freddy attacks you are

Freddy Krueger (Robert Englund) in his original dark mode (*A Nightmare On Elm Street*, New Line, 1984).

established here, since it's shown that what he does to you in the dream world will also happen in the waking world. Upon killing Tina, his first victim in the franchise, he slashes her chest in her nightmare. In the real world, her body is lifted up into the air, floating above the bed. The claw marks from the dream then appear on her body, mirroring the dream wounds. Later in the film, we are shown another character, Rod, who is strangled by a bed sheet. In the real world, Freddy is able to make the sheet move on its own and wrap around his neck. So, we see two things: he can influence what happens in reality, and wounds inflicted in dreams also occur outside them.

Our protagonists include Nancy Thompson, whose mother and father helped in the killing of Krueger, and she's played by Heather Langenkamp, who was just starting out in acting. Nancy has a sort of boyfriend named Glen who lives across the street, played by Johnny Depp in his very first film role. Shortly after, he'd land a spot in *Platoon*, and then go one to huge success on television with *21 Jump Street*, and then go on to make a few other random movies that you may possibly have heard of. Genre vet John Saxon also appears as Nancy's father, basically defining the rest of his career. There's pretty much no way to see Saxon in anything and not say, "Oh, hey. There's Nancy's dad."

Of course, the biggest role to fill was that of Freddy himself, and there's an interesting "what if" in that David Warner was originally cast in the role. He was all lined up to take up the glove, and even did some makeup tests, but ultimately had to drop out due to some scheduling issues. After Warner left, Craven was convinced to talk to Robert Englund, who had won over the casting director during an audition for an entirely different film. At the time, Englund was appearing on the TV show *V,* playing a drastically different type of character. He took the role of Freddy mainly because he was able to fit it into his shooting hiatus on the show, and obviously was not expecting it to turn into the phenomenon that it did.

In setting up the time frame of the world, there really isn't anything that reveals when this entry is set outside of a few throwaway moments. At one point, Nancy watches the original *Evil Dead* on TV, which came out in 1981, indicating that it takes place at some point after that, although I'm not quite sure the film was released on the rental market, and you can guarantee that it wasn't being aired on regular channels, considering that cable wasn't widespread at that point, so the number of places in which she could've been viewing that film are pretty limited. There's also a quick flash of license plate showing a registration expiration of December of 1984, so it would most likely be set sometime in that year.

The ending of the film involves Nancy realizing that she is able to pull Freddy out of the dream world and into reality by holding on to him as she wakes up. After a struggle, the film casts doubt on whether she's even awakened, and she uses a technique discussed earlier in order to take away the power that she had given him. By not being afraid of him, he is rendered powerless, but a final scene reveals that her victory is only temporary.

The way the ending is shot creates a lot of questions, casting doubt on whether it takes place in the real world or in dreams. After bringing him out, Freddy still seems to have some sort of reality manipulation and is still remarkably resistant to damage and pain. It can be theorized that Nancy never manages to get him, and the entire finale of the film is still within her dream.

No one expected the film to be a huge success, and certainly no one anticipated the place it would take in horror history. Surprisingly, it even received a number of positive reviews from critics, praising the film's ambience and dreamlike elements and crediting it for stepping out of the standard slasher formula that was defining the genre at the time. It had a pretty modest $1 million budget and was only given a limited release, playing in a mere 165 theaters in its opening weekend. Even with this small number of venues, it still pulled in $1.2 million in its debut, instantly earning back its production budget. As its reputation grew over the next few weeks, more and more theaters were added, until eventually it collected $25 million across the US and added in another

$32 million worldwide, adding up to a colossal $57 million total.[1] It would go on to cement New Line as a legitimate film studio and change the shape of horror for the next decade or so.

And so, to the surprise of exactly no one, a sequel was ordered. Several versions of the script were ordered, both of which shied away from the dream-world aspects of the first film, instead delving into the idea that Freddy would possess someone in the waking world. One of the scripts would be about a pregnant woman whose fetus Krueger would begin to control. This version didn't go over very well with one of the New Line producers, who was pregnant at the time, so they went with the other version. That one focuses on Freddy taking over the form of a teenage boy. Craven was offered the chance to direct again, but he hated the script, and so he declined. This allowed Jack Sholder to step in, fresh off of a film entitled *Alone in the Dark*. One year later, in 1985, *A Nightmare on Elm Street 2: Freddy's Revenge* arrived.

The sequel marked a drastic change for practically every aspect of the series. Nancy doesn't return, and Robert Englund as Freddy Krueger is the only returning cast member, unless you count the infamous Elm Street house.

Most of the dream elements were cast aside, instead focusing on the possession storyline, with Freddy opting to murder in the real world through the use of a proxy in the form of Jesse, whose family has just moved into the Thompson house. While there are dreamlike aspects to the overall story, the line is blurred between any of those sequences being dreams or just an altered perspective of what Jesse is enacting under Krueger's control. While the audience is seeing Freddy slash his victims, it's implied that this is just Jesse doing these deeds while wearing the glove, and our view is the way the teenager is experiencing it.

Midway through the film, Jesse and his girlfriend discover Nancy's diary in the back of the closet and start reading her entries about the events of the first film. They mention that they're from five years ago, marking a gap between the two films, and they also place those entries in March. If the first film was actually set in 1984, then this one would be in 1989, four years into the future from the release date.

The look of Freddy remains pretty consistent, with a continuation of the dark tone that would soon go away. His abilities remain similar to the first film, although he seems to have more influence on the waking world, assuming that what we're seeing on-screen is not a dream itself, which is actually questionable. An interesting question to raise is how exactly Freddy was able to take over Jesse in the first place. Given that it does allow him a conduit into the real world, able to reach some victims that might normally be out of his reach, it's a little surprising that he never thinks to use this tactic again.

Much has already been said about the film's gay subtext, and while it's taken its place as a film within the LGBTQ+ spectrum, the filmmaker's intentions have never been solidified. Sholder has outright denied any knowledge of the subtext, and screenwriter David Chaskin has both denied and confirmed the idea. The film's lead, Mark Patton, blames the film and its homoerotic storyline for destroying his acting career, but it has become a staple among the gay community, although this is a little curious, because the storyline seems to have a vaguely homophobic viewpoint. Freddy, interpreted as Jesse's repressed homosexuality, is viewed as the monster that he has to keep locked away. When it escapes, it hurts the people around him, damaging his family and friends. It's only through the love of his girlfriend, Lisa, that he's able to overcome the "evil" and return life as normal. Chaskin has partially confirmed this interpretation by stating that he intended to capitalize on the growing homophobia among young men in the '80s. Regardless, it has been embraced as an early form of representation, as many gay horror fans were able to see themselves in the character.

As mentioned, Freddy is eventually destroyed in the end of the film, through a kiss, again draining his power. Although the film represents it as a "power of love" scenario, it's more likely a scenario more in line with the first film. Since it was established that Freddy feeds off belief and the power that the dreamer gives him, it's possible that Jesse just stopped

Part 2's very serious Krueger (Robert Englund) (*A Nightmare on Elm Street 2: Freddy's Revenge*, New Line, 1985).

fearing Krueger. Like Nancy did, Jesse may have taken away his power, allowing his physical form to emerge and dispel Freddy's. Much like the first film, however, the final scene reveals him to still be active, setting the stage for more.

It was released in an unusual time slot, debuting immediately after Halloween, and went up against several action films. The second film was not the overwhelming smash that the first one was, but it was still highly profitable, making $30 million.[2] Even with a significantly increased budget of $3 million, that still equaled a big success, and plans to continue the series moved forward.

A Nightmare on Elm Street 3: Dream Warriors arrived two years later, but it very narrowly escaped never happening. After *Freddy's Revenge* was disliked by critics and audiences alike, New Line was skeptical about continuing the series. However, Wes Craven decided to return to cowrite the screenplay for the third film, with the intention of it being a finale to the series. Because of this, the company decided to go ahead with it, and asked Craven to also return to the directing chair. Due to his commitment to making *Deadly Friend*, he was unable to do, so they brought on Chuck Russell, in his directorial debut.

Craven was then tasked with the challenge of figuring out where to take the story. Thankfully, unlike the slasher films that were rooted in mostly real-world scenarios, Freddy was supernatural, so bringing him back could be an easier task. Craven's first idea was to really change up the game and do a sort of meta-commentary, having Freddy invade the "real" world with the actors of the series playing themselves. New Line would dismiss this as "too high concept," but it was an idea that Craven would return to several years later.

Also, both Robert Englund and John Saxon would try their hands at delivering a script for the film. Saxon's was a prequel, which would reveal that Krueger was originally innocent and had been set up for his crimes. In his version, Freddy is taking revenge against those who wrongfully killed him by coming after their children, painting him in a slightly more sympathetic light. Englund's version was a more standard sequel, featuring the older sister of Tina, from the first film, returning to Springwood to find out the truth of Tina's death. There, she would face off against the dream killer, utilizing dream journals to map out the fantasy world in order to conceal weapons to use against him.

Instead of either of those, the final product would be written by Wes Craven and Bruce Wagner, with the decision made to shift the focus away from Freddy facing off against a singular opponent, and instead have him fight against a group. *Dream Warriors* was born.

The third film marks a return to the feeling of the first film, once again heavily featuring the dream sequence concepts to play with what is reality and what is not. It introduces a vital new character, Kristen, who is being targeted by a returned Krueger. After being made to look like she's attempted suicide, she's institutionalized with a group of teenagers with similar dreams. Nancy returns as an intern there, immediately recognizing that Freddy is back and targeting them.

Heather Langenkamp returns as Nancy, and she's joined by both Englund and Saxon, adding to the feeling that this film is actually the "true" sequel to the original, and the second film can be discounted.

While discussing her backstory, Nancy gives us our timeframe for the film, telling the group that her friends were killed by Freddy six years ago. That places this entry at six years after the first film, and just one year after the second. If we're still assuming that the first film was in 1984, then that would actually make this one set in 1990, a few years later than the actual release date.

It's never really discussed exactly how the dream killer returns after the last film, and in fact, the events of *Freddy's Revenge* are essentially ignored. It can be assumed, much like the final scene of that one showed, that Freddy was never really vanquished in it, and this is just a continuation of his reign of terror. It's possible that those finales represent his strength being taken away, rendering him temporarily powerless. It would then take time for him to regain his strength, allowing him to once again tap into the dreams of others.

In spite of the omission of *Freddy's Revenge*, there are quite a few continuity points in this one, and some alterations to the characters. As stated, Nancy returns, and her character has gone into the study of psychology, seemingly focusing on dreams, which is pretty appropriate. Her dad also makes an appearance, now wearing a security guard uniform and drinking heavily, with the implication being that he began drinking after the death of his wife and either quit the police or was fired. Speaking of Nancy's mom, she's mentioned again and is said to have died in her sleep. This doesn't necessarily contradict what was said in the last film, that she killed herself, as that could just be the alterations in the story that were made by a high school student as would likely happen in the telling and retelling of local legends. It's also possible that both stories are true, and that she did kill herself, but used a bottle of pills in order to do so, making Nancy's statement about dying in her sleep also true. What neither account clears up is whether her mother actually died at the end of the last film, or if the whole "sinking into the bed" scenario was just a dream. It's never really stated whether Freddy killed her, or if she truly did end up killing herself.

Krueger himself accounts for the biggest deviation from what had come before. Instead of being the dark, vicious slasher that was depicted earlier, he's portrayed with a lighter sensibility here. After killing his victims, he begins delivering a number of one-liners, creating a comedic element to the character. His method of killing has also become more elaborate, with a greater emphasis on his reality-distortion abilities. Over the course of the film, he turns himself into a bathroom sink, a giant snake, a television set, and a set of mirrored duplicates. He also now seems to have some sort of control of his victims' bodies as well, turning one of them into a marionette using his veins, and animating a former junkie's track marks into a bunch of hungry little mouths. This turning point for the character marked his transformation from a dark and scary monster, beginning his path to the wisecracking pop cultural icon that he would soon become.

This film also begins to tell Krueger's backstory, an element that will be further fleshed out later in the series. Here, we meet the ghost of Amanda Krueger, Freddy's mother, who tells that she was trapped in an asylum overnight and horribly raped by one hundred of the patients, fathering the future psychopath. Somewhat importantly, at the end of the film, we are shown her gravestone, and it indicates the year of her death to be 1968.

The finale takes place in both the real world and the dream realm, with Nancy and the kids, now using powers that they discover with their fantasies, fighting Freddy in their dreams, while Doctor Neil seeks out the burned skeletal remains of Krueger in order to bury them and place

TV Freddy's (Robert Englund) prime time kill (with Penelope Sudrow) (*A Nightmare on Elm Street 3: Dream Warriors,* New Line, 1987).

his spirit at rest. After the deaths of several characters, including Nancy's dad and Nancy herself, the bones are finally laid to rest and Freddy is destroyed. And, of course, even though Craven had considered his script to be a final entry, the final shot does indeed hint that more is to come.

Now, because of Craven's renewed involvement, the budget had been increased to about $4.5 million, so the stakes were a bit higher, but the gamble paid off. *Dream Warriors* debuted in the number 1 spot, knocking out the box office juggernaut of *Platoon*, and scoring a solid $8.8 million opening weekend. When all was said and done, it pulled in close to $45 million in the US,[3] earning back ten times its budget and received a number of positive reviews. Fans were also very pleased, and it's considered to be one of the best in the series, even today.

With the series reinvigorated, New Line was now all in on the character, quickly moving forward with the next entry. Wes Craven was again approached to write the film, but when his idea involved time travel within dreams, they decided to go another direction. So, instead of *A Nightmare on Elm Street 4: Time to Dream* (or something), we got 1988's *A Nightmare on Elm Street 4: The Dream Master*. Renny Harlin was tapped to direct, fresh off his cult horror hit, *Prison*. Based on the increased success of the third film, he was given an extra couple million dollars to play with, as well as a dramatically increased promotional push.

Some of the key cast members of the last one were not included here, including Dr. Neil Gordon and Nancy, of course, but several survivors were. The surviving Elm Street kid trio of Kristen, Joey, and Kincaid all returned, although only two of them were played by the same actors. Patricia Arquette was not interested in being known as a horror actress and declined to return, instead being replaced with Tuesday Knight.

Alongside the returning trio, it introduces a group of new characters, including Lisa Wilcox as Alice and Danny Hassel as Dan. They play high school friends of Kristen's, along with several other new characters.

The film follows the three some time after the end of the last film. They're back in high school, and have clearly been there for some time. Joey's hair has drastically increased in length and Kristen has a whole new group of friends, including a boyfriend that she's been with for some time. The amount of time is never clearly stated. Kristen's fears of Freddy returning turn out to be well founded, as he reanimates and starts killing once again. The method of his revival is perhaps the most notorious element in the film, since in Kincaid's dream, a dog walks over to Freddy's grave and urinates fire onto it, causing the Krueger to reform out of his skeleton. It's pretty special, and probably misunderstood. Quite a few viewers take it as a sort of literal thing that happens. That Freddy is resurrected because a dog peed on his grave. It's important to realize that this occurs in a dream, and the dog is merely a dream construct version of Kincaid's dog. It's a surreal dream image that Krueger has conjured up to play with the big guy's fears.

This one establishes some new parts of Freddy lore in that he is unable to enter the dreams of just anyone. He specifically has the ability to enter only the dreams of Elm Street children, and cannot just appear anywhere. Since Kristen is the last of them, he tries to use her dream ability to bring him new victims, but then also kills her. For some reason, Kristen also passes her powers to Alice, which seems a little short-sighted on both of their parts. Since she was his only access to other victims, it's not really a good move for him to kill her. But, on Kristen's part, if she didn't pass her powers on, Freddy would be stuck with no way to enter other dreams. But since she did, he starts using Alice as his conduit, tapping into her friends' dreams and picking them off, one by one.

It also introduces the concept of Dream Masters. It seems that Freddy is one of them, and Alice is another. The job of the Masters is to guard the dream gates: one positive and one negative. It would seem that Freddy protects the bad dream gate, whereas Alice is supposed to protect the good dreams. There really isn't much information about the roles given in the film, and the tiny bit of exposition about Dream Masters was actually deleted. The concept is never again brought up in the films after this, as well.

Freddy's persona has officially transitioned here, and the dark specter of the first two films is completely gone, replaced by the wisecracking punster that the third film introduced. Every kill is now riddled with one-liners, and his guises have taken on a much sillier tone. To match this, there's an odd disparity with the rules of how his killings work. Unlike how it was depicted in the first film, here the wounds inflicted in dreams do not appear in reality. Kincaid is stabbed directly in the chest with the finger knives, and appears to only suffer a heart attack in the waking world. Freddy drains a character of life, leaving her dream form a withered husk, but her actual form merely has a fatal asthma attack. He also transforms a girl into a giant roach and crushes her in a roach motel, but the specifics of how that translates into reality is never shown. (I bet it's pretty gross, though.)

Oddly enough, the characters return to the Elm Street house, which was only present in the last film in dreams. Here, we're shown that in the real world, it's abandoned and in a state of disrepair. This

MTV Freddy (Robert Englund) beginning to embrace his sillier side (*A Nightmare on Elm Street 4: The Dream Master,* New Line, 1988).

would seem to imply that Jesse's family moved out shortly after the events of the second film, and it's been empty since. Since this film is possibly a year or so after the last one, that would make a two-year difference between the second film and this, which seems a pretty short time frame for the house to reach that level of dilapidation. It's possible that this one is meant to be set further into the future than two years, but it's also possible that Freddy's effect on the real world is starting to bleed through, making the house closer to its dream representation.

Near the end of the film, there's a scene in which Alice goes to a movie theater, and there are several movie posters up. One of them is clearly an inside joke, since it's for Harlin's film, *Prison,* but the other is for the John Waters film *Hairspray.* That came out in 1988, which would seem to be a sort of indication of the year, but it's possible that the theater is running older films. It raises the question of which is inaccurate, the first film's license plate sticker or this one's movie poster, but there is still no definitive answer.

After killing off most of the cast, there is a final showdown between the Dream Masters in the dream world, with Alice finally remembering an old nursery rhyme about her role. It contains the line "evil will see itself and it shall die," which inspires her to hold up a large mirror, showing Freddy his reflection. Sure enough, this seems to work, as the souls that are trapped with him start to fight back, tearing him apart to free themselves and killing Krueger, although the final shots of the film obviously let us know that his condition is merely temporary.

At the time of the film's release, Freddymania had fully taken over, with the character reaching his pop cultural high point. Krueger was everywhere, and the perception of him as a villain shifted to him being someone that the audience was rooting for. This new interpretation of the character all but took over the franchise, and this entry was the most evident victim of that. It's often referred to as the "MTV Freddy" movie, and is frequently blamed for fully converting Krueger into the punchline he'd become.

Based on the success of *Dream Warriors*, the fourth film's budget had been increased to $6.5 million, which was more than double that of the first two films combined. Another risk was taken by giving the film a summer release, albeit a late summer one, placing up against studio blockbusters. The chance was worth taking, since it had a massive opening weekend and easily took the number 1 spot. Its debut brought in close to $13 million, and it would end its run with just under $50 million, the highest-grossing entry of the series at that point.[4]

Around the same time, to capitalize on the popularity of the character, a TV series was launched, entitled *Freddy's Nightmares*. It launched in October 1988, just a few short months after the fourth film's release, and ran for two seasons. Concerned that the show would become repetitive with the killer simply stalking victims week after week, the decision was made to turn the show into an anthology, with new stories and characters each week. Over the course of 44 episodes, Freddy only really factored into eight of them, with him acting as more of a Crypt Keeper character for all the rest. He would generally appear in the introductions and epilogues of each story, setting up and then closing out the events. The episodes that did actually contain our killer would mostly be self-contained tales, although the exception was the very first one, which would actually flash back to Krueger's death. It detailed him being released from custody and eventually chased and killed by the parents. The continuity of this episode is questionable, due to a number of factors. First off, it's clearly set in the '80s, based on the fashions and technologies visible. Considering that the Springwood Slasher's death was in 1968, there's a big discrepancy with the time period. There's also the fact that we see all of the parents involved in the revenge killing, and Nancy's parents are not featured among them, nor are any of the other characters we know to be Elm Street parents. Based on this, I think it's pretty safe to say that this is an alternate version of events. There's also the possibility, given that Freddy is the host of the show and theoretically telling these stories, that he's giving a fictionalized take on his own story.

The show had its fair share of trouble, with a number of episodes having to be heavily edited to remove some of the more violent and titillating content for syndicated consumption. It received a decent amount of criticism from parent groups, who felt the show was too much for the airwaves and lobbied to have it taken off the schedules.

Freddy's powers were handled pretty differently in the show, which is fitting considering that he's more of an omniscient narrator than direct participant. He's shown to be far more powerful, with a wider variety of reality-altering abilities. Plus, although he's not directly featured in a large number of episodes, there's an implication that his influence is the cause of many of them, hinting at a power level that hadn't yet been seen in the films.

The craziest thing about the TV show is that it was canceled after two seasons. Normally, this would be due to low ratings, but that wasn't the case here. *Freddy's Nightmares* was actually performing quite well, and had solid numbers. But after the first season received such a large volume of complaints, the creators pared back the violent content for the second, which came with a budget slash as well. After fans vehemently complained about these changes, Warner Brothers decided that the show wasn't worth the hassle and ceased production.

There was no such hesitancy with the film series. After the huge numbers the fourth film did, it was clear that a fifth was in the pipeline. Very quickly, 1989 was blessed with *A Nightmare on Elm Street 5: The Dream Child*, with Stephen Hopkins taking the director role. Before this, he had only directed the Australian horror film *Dangerous Game*, but would later go on to be a part of creating the television shows *24*, *Californication*, and many others.

The scriptwriting process would be particularly tumultuous here, with revisions being made again and again; the Writer's Guild would eventually have to step in to determine who would get the actual credit for writing the film. Ultimately, it was decided that Leslie Bohem would get the core screenplay credit, while writers Craig Spector and John Skipp, who handled the bulk of the revisions, would get a "story by" credit. The majority of the story would actually be Bohem's concept for Part 2, *Freddy's Revenge*, since she was the one who had originally pitched the possessed pregnancy script.

All three of the surviving characters, Alice and her father and Dan, returned for the next entry. The film embraced the notion that the audience for the films has been growing up and getting older, and decided to focus on Alice graduating high school and dealing with pregnancy. Because fetuses are in a near constant dream state, Freddy is able to access it and use it to tap into Alice's abilities and enter into more nightmares.

The beginning of the film finally gives us our solid date to shape the timeline of the entire series. As Alice and her new group of friends are graduating, they're wearing tassels with the number 89 on them. Also, behind them, is a large banner congratulating the class of 1989, so that becomes our year. It's the first intentional and overt date in the entire series so far, and it becomes the true anchor point. With that in mind, we can back trace the previous films. We can use that Hairspray poster to place *Dream Master* in 1988, one year earlier, and give one additional year behind that for *Dream Warriors*, placing that one in 1987. Since we know that that's a year after Part 2, *Freddy's Revenge* takes place in 1986, with the original film occurring in 1981, five years prior. The only issues that occur with this are the license plate sticker, which is a small, inconsequential detail, and the *Evil Dead* on TV. Again, we can assume that in the Freddy Universe, that film came out a little earlier and was playing on TV screens in 1981.

There is actually a considerable amount of continuity between the fourth and fifth films, with both the characters and the abilities of the dreamers. Freddy still needs to use Alice to access other minds, only this time he's able to use the child to do it. Alice and Dan both return, although Dan is killed early on in the film. Interestingly, Alice remains the only character to survive multiple battles with Freddy, since every other returning character was killed off in subsequent entries.

Story-wise, Freddy uses the child to kill off Alice's crew, using a variety of increasingly absurd methods to do so. He turns Dan into a weird, techno-organic motorcycle thing, transforms into a chef, and at one point rides a skateboard before turning into SuperFreddy, a super hero (villain?) version of himself. It should be noted that the makeup design has drastically been altered for this entry, becoming more simplified, as Robert Englund requested a more streamlined look to avoid spending countless hours in the makeup chair. The end result is a more rubbery, slightly more cartoonish appearance for the killer. This does actually match his enhanced persona here, since his sillier aspects are leaned into very heavily, completely eliminating the scarier aspects of the villain.

This one delves a little deeper into the Amanda Krueger storyline, flashing back to actually show the incident in which she is locked in with the insane inmates. She once again becomes a character as well, appearing in a younger form than she did in *Dream Warriors*, guiding Alice to defeat Freddy. After they are able to find her body, Amanda is free to reclaim Freddy, reabsorbing him into her being and taking on the challenge of keeping him from wreaking havoc. It ends with Alice having given birth, moving on, even though there's a slight hint that Freddy

Part 5's much less serious Super Freddy (Michael Bailey Smith with Joe Seely) (*A Nightmare on Elm Street 5: The Dream Child*, New Line, 1989).

can return. It's unclear at this point if Alice has retained Kristen's powers, or if they have passed on to her child, Jacob; the two characters are never seen or mentioned in the film series again. They were, however, brought back in several comic book follow-ups.

A small detail that adds to the overall timeline is the revelation that Amanda committed suicide upon hearing about her child's acquittal, blaming herself for the evil unleashed. This is fairly notable as we were previously given her death year as 1968. Since we know that the vigilante parents killed Freddy very shortly after his release, we can place his physical death in '68 as well. This means that after being given powers by the dream demons, he would have spent 13 years building up his power base and skill level to actually activate his abilities to gain revenge.

Even though the character was still hugely popular, and the budget of the film was again increased, this time to $8 million, it failed to make an impact at the box office. Once again given a late summer release, reviews for the film were overwhelmingly negative, and fan reaction was as well. Placing third in its opening weekend, behind the family comedy *Parenthood* and the opening weekend of *The Abyss*, it only managed to do $8 million, a pretty dramatic drop from the fourth film's take, and a small decrease from that of the third film. After all was said and done, it only brought in $22 million, less than half of what the fourth film made, and was deemed a box office flop.[5]

With popularity waning, and New Line wanting to move on to

other projects, it was decided to end the franchise. In 1991, they boldly declared their intentions with *Freddy's Dead: The Final Nightmare*, a movie that would kill off the villain once and for all. As you know, with horror films, if you call your film the final chapter, you must stick to it and not make any more.

Rachel Talalay was hired to direct, her directorial debut, although she had served as a producer on the fourth film. She also produced *Hairspray*, which is likely why that film's poster was shown in the movie theater. It was the first time that a woman had taken the reins in the franchise, and remains the only time.

One of the earliest incarnations of the script actually came from horror legend Peter Jackson. His version was a pretty unique take on the concept, with a film entitled *Nightmare on Elm Street 6: Dream Lover*. His take made use of the fact that, in reality, Freddy was not seen as scary anymore, and was considered a bit of joke. His fictional Springwood mirrored that, as Krueger was essentially powerless after the events of the fifth film, and was no longer feared by the town's residents, a fact that kept him from being able to harm anyone. Because of this, teenagers would intentionally take sleeping pills in order to enter the dream world and beat up the weakened killer. But eventually Freddy would turn the tables, regaining his powers and becoming a threat once again. It's not known why New Line passed on this concept.

Although the final film doesn't carry over any characters from the last film, it originally did. Both Alice and Jacob were included and the film would start with them. However, Freddy would pretty quickly give Alice the glove treatment. This version also featured the return of several of the characters from *Dream Warriors*, brought forth by Jacob's powers to serve as some sort of guardian team for the dream world. Talalay hated this concept and had it eliminated, and shortly after, the Alice portion was dropped entirely. Jacob's bits were actually retained in script, although he was changed to be an entirely new and unconnected character, referred to as John Doe.

The opening of the sixth film opens a huge can of worms for the timeline. A graphic is shown on-screen announcing that it's set "ten years from now," and goes on to detail that in the gap between movies, Krueger returned and killed off all of the children of Springwood, leaving behind a town of adults only. It's not made clear what their intention is with this time frame. Is it meant to be ten years from the time frame of the last film, making it set in 1999? Is it ten years from the time of release, placing it in 2001? Or does it possibly mean that it's ten years from a literal now, so it's ten years of the future of whenever you're watching it? Judging from the clothing, technology, and cars, it doesn't seem to be that far removed and developed: coincidentally, it looks like 1991.

Since it was intended to be the finale of the series, a lot of storyline issues were discussed, although several previous points were summarily discarded. One of these is the limitation of entering dreams. Instead of needing Alice or Jacob to enter dreams, Freddy can seemingly go into whoever's mind that he pleases. The impression given is that he has killed enough people and collected enough power that his abilities keep on growing and expanding, even allowing him some sort of control over the real world as well. The only stipulation given is that he's unable to leave the town of Springwood at all. He is trapped there, and can only leave through the power of a blood relative.

Oh, yeah. Freddy has a kid now. In order to give him a blood relative, a backstory was created in which at one point, Krueger was married and had a child during the time that he was also acting as the Springwood Slasher. The information is hinted at throughout the film and solidified when our group of wayward teens and their caretaker find their way back to the little Ohio town. There, they discover all of the insane adult denizens, and the local school teacher informs them that back in 1966, they took Krueger's child away from him. Interestingly enough, one of the teens that are with them is convinced that he is the lost offspring, although he's either in his late teens or early 20s, which would make the time frame extremely wrong. If the film is taking place in the late '90s, the child would be over 30 years old, nearing 40, which John Doe clearly is not.

The child turns out to be Maggie, the teen's caretaker, and her backstory is fully fleshed out, revealing a bit more of the timeline of events. We're shown a flashback to her as a little girl in her back yard, interacting with her still-human father. When her mother discovers Mr. Krueger's extracurricular deeds, he strangles her to keep her quiet in front of young Maggie. Even though she promises to not tell anyway, she does, and it's this tipoff that eventually leads to the capture of the Springwood Slasher, and causing them to take her away from him. We know that happens in '66, and we also know that Krueger dies in '68, which lets us know that the arrest and trial process took a full two years to complete.

Most of these flashbacks occur during the film's finale, which was shown in 3D format in its initial release. This is presented as a trip through Freddy's mind, as Maggie is aided by wearing actual 3D glasses, which is not the slightest bit silly. And it's not made even sillier when viewed in a non-3D format, either. Through these sequences, we are also witness to other moments in young Freddy's life, such as his teasing by fellow school students when he is a young boy, calling him the "son of hundred maniacs." They do so after he crushes a frog with a hammer, showing his evil intentions began early on. We also see him as a teenager, fighting back against an abusive foster father played by Alice Cooper, and killing him. It's unclear if this is his first murder, but the film seems to be suggesting this. We also see the moment that his human form is murdered, this time including the dream demons.

This is the other big addition to the lore within the film. It is now postulated that Freddy's dream abilities were actually granted to him by ancient creatures known as the dream demons, which are floating, wormlike creatures that appear to him before death. Coincidentally, a doctor who works at the shelter has a poster of them on his wall, and is fully knowledgeable about their lore even before he's aware of Freddy's presence, which seems like it would be pretty unlikely. Krueger immediately begins talking about them as soon as he meets the guy, too, which is a little strange. This dream killer, who has never once mentioned dream demons before, suddenly starts being really chatty about them around the one guy in the series who just so happens to have a poster of them on his wall. It's said that these demons would seek out especially depraved human beings to act as their agents, sowing chaos in the waking world, but there's no mention of their actions outside of Freddy, such as whether they had any agents before him, and the heroes aren't concerned about the notion of them choosing someone else to carry on their work once they've killed Krueger.

Freddy (Robert Englund) sporting the Power Glove (*Freddy's Dead: The Final Nightmare*, New Line, 1991).

Another element that contradicts the previous entries is the teenagers' ability to enter each other's dreams. Partway through the film, as Freddy is after a character named Spencer, played by Breckin Meyer, several other of the youths decide to try to save him. John Doe asks Tracy, another of the troubled teens, to hit him over the head to knock him out. She does so, and he is able to merge into Spencer's dream. Tracy then does the same herself, using techniques that she claims to have learned from Doc. This is an odd addition since the previous films had established that people were only able to enter into each other's dreams through the use of either Kristen or Alice's abilities, but it can possibly be attributed to the weakening of the walls of the dream reality.

Another minor element of history in the series is the inclusion of Johnny Depp, returning to the franchise for the first time since the original film. He's not appearing as Glen; he's just making a cameo on television, possibly as himself. He's doing an anti-drug PSA, which is then interrupted by Freddy. Besides this, there's a number of other unusual cameos throughout, although they're unrelated to the previous entries. Both Roseanne and Tom Arnold appear briefly, and as mentioned before, so does Alice Cooper.

They do manage to tie into previous continuity, as they bring back a concept from the very first movie in order to facilitate their defense. They intend to bring Freddy out of the dream world and into the real one, where he will be vulnerable. Similar to the first one, after they do so, the rules are pretty gray. At first it seems as if he's been reverted to a human, unburned state, completely mortal once again, but this soon turns out to be a trick and he reverts back to his standard form. Next, he's seen crawling around on the ceiling, dropping down on Maggie from above. Both of these actions indicate he still has some reality-altering powers in the waking world, but their extent appears to be limited. He can still be injured, as when his hand is broken, he isn't able to just restore himself, and his fingers remain damaged, as well as being vulnerable to being stabbed with his own glove and then blown up with that convenient dynamite that all youth shelters inevitably have. As he explodes, we see the dream demons leaving his body, suggesting that he is no longer their agent, and is truly dead.

The film's release was a bit of a mixed bag. Since it was the intended final entry, the budget was slightly boosted to around $10 million, and with the hype, expectations were high. The opening weekend looked to be a big success with a $13 million take, but didn't maintain those numbers and finished its run at just under $35 million.[6] Critics universally panned the film and audience reaction was pretty unfavorable, and it's oft considered to be the worst entry in the series.

As expected, the notion of a "final chapter" in a horror series proved to be an empty promise, since more entries would follow. There was only a three-year gap between *Freddy's Dead* and 1994's *New Nightmare*, but as it turns out, the idea of Freddy Krueger being killed off was actually something that would hold true. Being the 10th anniversary of the original film, Wes Craven decided to return to the franchise to both write and direct the new entry, bringing the dream killer back to the silver screen.

His concept, however, would turn the series on its burned-up ear. Instead of continuing the existing continuity, Craven introduced an idea that he had intended to use way back in the third film, which involved Freddy attacking actors in the real world making a sequel to *A Nightmare on Elm Street*. He returned to this for the seventh entry, setting the film in Hollywood and utilizing a number of actors from the franchise, playing themselves. Heather Langenkamp would return, playing a slightly fictionalized version of herself, as would Robert Englund, who took on dual roles as himself as well as Freddy. John Saxon also came back, also playing himself, with Wes Craven and Robert Shaye also appearing.

The interesting notion introduced here is that the killer is not actually Freddy, but an ancient demon that has taken on his form. It seems that the creature is able to be contained for periods of time within fictions, and was trapped within the form of Freddy on film. When they decided to kill off the character, ending the series, the demon was set loose, still retaining the shape that it had inhabited, to haunt the cast and crew.

Since the entity is not the exact same as we've been watching for the previous six films, it doesn't follow the same rules. Most of the characteristics of Freddy are still intact, but there are a few things that are not consistent. This version of the demon seems to be able to impact reality a bit more, and is not as reliant on the victim being asleep. A good example of this is the babysitter of Heather's son, Dylan. Although it is shown that the little boy goes under, due to sedatives that were given to him, the babysitter is wide awake, yet Freddy is able to kill her anyway, apparently using the sleeping Dylan to be able to do so.

The timeframe of the film is a little confusing, as the beginning shows us that Los Angeles has been subject to a series of earthquakes, and the news compares them to a recent large quake in the Northridge, California, area. This is an event that occurred in the real world, and happened in January 1994, so it would seem as if the film was set a short time after that. A little later, while interviewing Heather on a television show, the host tells her that the 10th anniversary of the original film is coming up soon. The first one came out in the latter half of 1984, so it would seem as if this was set sometime between January and November of 1994. The weather's pretty pleasant but it's Los Angeles, so that could basically be at any time of the year.

This is thrown into question at the very end of the story. After Heather and Dylan defeat Freddy in their dream, trapping him and burning him, apparently destroying the demon, they discover a completed version of the script. Throughout the film, it has been shown that Wes Craven was actually writing the screenplay based on dreams that he was having, and these events would then happen in the real world, so his writing process and the scenes we see in the film occur almost simultaneously. This is shown earlier on as Robert Englund states that Wes had told him that he was up to the point in which "Dylan tried to reach god." We have just witnessed this happening to the characters, showing that the script and the film events happen together. So at the end, when Heather flips through the pages, we see marks denoting revisions that are dated November 1993. The revisions are shown on a script page detailing events of the film that had taken place about two days prior, and since revisions are done after the initial writing process, there's no way that this could have occurred before that date. That places this film in November of '93, which notes that in this fictionalized version of the universe, the Northridge quake occurred at an earlier point. This doesn't contradict the TV host, as he states that the 10th anniversary is coming up, which could just be referring to the changing from '93 to '94, the actual anniversary year. An interesting aspect of this is that technically, this film takes place earlier than *Freddy's Dead*, although that contradiction doesn't matter, as it's set in a separate universe and continuity.

Again, since this is a different Freddy, there were a number of changes to the established characteristics. The most obvious was his personality. He is no longer the wisecracking, pun-loving, comedic killer that we put up with for the past three films. He's returned to the original style, taking only when necessary, and remaining in the shadows for the majority of the time, acting more sinister. He has also switched from using more elaborate, reality-altering killing methods, switching back to utilizing his glove more frequently. The alterations to his look match this shift, as the coloring of his trademark sweater has darkened, looking less garish than before. The burns on his skin are drastically different, looking more like open gaps on his face than random burn marks, and his eyes have turned pure white with black pupils. Another drastic change is the complete redo of his glove. Instead of an actual, simple glove with blades attached to the fingers, it features a more bio-mechanic look, with long bone-like links to wrap around each finger. It gives the impression of his fingers actually being the blades more than before. Finally, he's taken to wearing a long trench coat, hiding his silhouette more and keeping him hidden, as well as some stylish leather pants.

The ending of the film once again features a final showdown between Freddy and Nancy, although technically this is the first time they face off. Since this is actually Heather Langenkamp fighting a demon in the form of Freddy, it's their first meeting. Here, stopping the evil is quite a bit easier, since they just have to trap him in a furnace and light it. This sets the demon on fire, killing it, and revealing its true visage, which looks ... uh ... not good.

New Nightmare was released in theaters on the same weekend as *Pulp Fiction*, which possibly affected its total box office, but it's also possible that audiences were just over the *Nightmare* series in general, especially since it was said to be done with it a few years earlier. Whatever the reason, it translated to low ticket sales, bringing in a mere $20 million worldwide,[7] the worst-performing entry in the series. On a brighter note for the film, it ended up receiving some of the more positive reviews over the course of the franchise, and has since gone on to become one of the fan favorites.

As a result of the seventh film's failure, and just a general lack of interest in the series in general, nothing happened with Freddy for

A creature in the shape of Freddy (Robert Englund with Tracy Middendorf) appears in a really bright green hat (*Wes Craven's New Nightmare*, New Line, 1994).

close to a decade. It was decided that the next time the character would appear would be in a crossover film, teaming him up with Jason Voorhees, but there were massive issues with the script and the studio's interest in making it. But things finally clicked, and in 2003, the epic battle commenced with *Freddy vs. Jason.*

Robert Englund would return, of course, and as detailed in the chapter on *Friday the 13th*, Jason would be recast, so fans would miss out on seeing the two most recognizable forms of their favorite slashers take each other on.

There's a considerable amount of Freddy continuity here, as the majority of the film takes place in Springwood. Unlike *Freddy's Dead*, the town is full of teenagers and children, and the general insanity of the adults there seems to have tapered off. It's explained that the elders in the town have erased all existence and mention of Freddy, completely hiding any knowledge of him from the children. Without anyone to fear him, Krueger loses all power, stripping him of his ability to enter the children's dreams. Any of the youth who happen to remember him are sent away to an institution and placed on Hypnocil, the drug from the third film. One of those teenagers mentions that he has been locked up there for the past four years, and it's later shown that he had been placed there after his brother was killed by Freddy, which tells us that the dream killer had been active about four years prior. Later in the film, a police chief mentions that the town has been peaceful for four years, backing up that number and indicating that Freddy has been inactive for that same time frame. There's a flashback to our lead girl's past involving the death of her mother, revealed to have been the work of Freddy, also said to be four years prior, again confirming that there were nightmare murders happening just a few short years ago.

As talked about in the *Friday the 13th* chapter, Freddy recruits Jason from hell in order to help him spread fear within Springwood, causing the townspeople to start talking about him again, giving him power. Unfortunately, the hockey-masked mammoth gets a little carried away, which leads to a face-off between the two in the real world.

During this showdown, a billboard is seen in the background advertising a group of condos that will open in spring of 2004. Again, as pointed out in the earlier chapter, this indicates the film is set in late 2003, which actually lines up with the timeline. Four years prior to that was 1999, which is one of the possible years for *Freddy's Dead* to have occurred. If Lori's mother and Mark's brother were killed shortly before the events of that film, that would match the talk of being four year later. It would seem that in '99, Freddy was killed by Maggie, draining him of whatever power he had stored up. Taking advantage of his weakened state, the town of Springwood was freed from whatever hold he had over them and devised the plan to erase him from their history. There's some discussion online about the possibility of *Freddy's Dead* taking place after *Freddy vs. Jason*, with Krueger using the power that he gains over the course of the film to wipe out Springwood and lead into the events of the earlier film. While this is a possibility, in the beginning of *FvJ*, while recounting his past exploits, we are shown snippets of *Freddy's Dead* in a montage, suggesting that those instances had indeed already occurred.

Freddy's general appearance in this one is closer to the stylings of the original films. He's reverted back to the classic sweater and pants look, and his facial scarring resembles his look from the third film. There is an interesting change late in the film, in the dream world, as Freddy takes on a more demonic countenance. His teeth are long and pointed, as are his ears, and his skin takes on a more reddish tint. This look is very short-lived, and when he is drawn out into the real world, he reverts back to his more standard appearance.

In the final fight of the film, Jason is arguably victorious, stabbing Freddy through the chest with his own arm, although Lori is the one to strike the killing blow, cutting off Krueger's head. Since this occurs in the real world, with the dream stalker being pulled out into the waking world, it essentially kills him. However, a final shot shows Jason emerging from the lake with Freddy's severed head in his hand, which gives a playful wink at the camera, indicating that he's not truly dead.

As I discussed in the earlier chapter, the film was a massive hit. It easily outperformed all of the other films, pulling in close to $115 million worldwide, and remains the largest opening weekend for the entire franchise at $36 million.[8]

The rather dramatic change in appearance of Demon Freddy (Robert Englund) (*Freddy vs. Jason*, New Line, 2003).

But outside of the aforementioned Freddy vs. Jason vs. Ash comic book series, there were no further continuations, and the character has had no further escapades in the movies. *Freddy vs. Jason* represents the final film portrayal of Krueger by Robert Englund.

Several years passed, and after successful remakes of the *Texas Chainsaw Massacre* and *Friday the 13th*, it was decided that it was time for a New Nightmare, just not *Wes Craven's New Nightmare*. No, it was time for a remake.

2010's *A Nightmare on Elm Street* would see first-time feature director Samuel Bayer take the chair, and for the first time, the role of Freddy would be played by someone other than Robert Englund. The part would instead go to Academy Award nominee Jackie Earle Haley, with a drastic makeup redesign that would favor a more realistic look for the burns. His take on the character was less jokey, and closer to the tone of the original film.

For the most part, the general plot structure would follow that of the first film, repeating several of the same story beats and characters. Oddly, although some characters would stay the same as they were previously presented, even maintaining their names, others would follow different story paths or just have new names. There really doesn't seem to be much rhyme or reason, with Tina's story matching the first, yet altering her name to Kris, and a new character named Quentin, who mostly has an original arc.

The most interesting notion that the remake introduces is the possibility that Freddy was innocent, and was unjustly killed by the parents. In this universe, he wasn't a child killer, and was instead accused of molesting the children of the preschool where he worked. After he's killed by a vigilante mob of parents, much like the original, the question

Remake Freddy (Jackie Earle Haley) goes back to the boiler room (*A Nightmare on Elm Street,*** New Line/Platinum Dunes, 2010).**

is brought up as to whether the children were lying, and the parents instead murdered an innocent man. Unfortunately, this bold choice is then just tossed aside when it turns out that he was indeed a child molester, an element that was implied in the original series, but never outright stated.

It also introduces a new wrinkle in the concept of micro napping. It seems that people who are extremely sleep deprived will have moments of dreaming while still awake, similar to hallucinations, and in these small fragments of time, Freddy has access to you. It ends up being a very minor part of the story, not really amounting to an impact on the overall plot.

Another confusing aspect to the film is the timeline, since it can't quite decide when it takes place. A number of dates are given in the film that all contradict each other. Early in the film, an obituary states that the character Dean was born in 1991, and was 19 years old when he died. That would imply that the film takes place in 2010, its year of release. Earlier, Kris discovers a series of boxes; one is marked "first grade–1996," and it's stated that the kids are all the same age. One curious thing about that is that if they were all 19, it seems a little unusual that they would all still be in high school, but it's also odd that Kris would have only been five when she went to first grade. We don't quite know what year she was born, so there's some flexibility there, but later on in the film, it's stated that they all were in the same preschool class from '94 to '95. That can match up with starting first grade in 1996 if her kindergarten year was from '95 to '96 and she was starting first grade in the fall of '96, but later on in the film, other obituaries are seem from other classmates who died, and they're all stated to be 17. If it were 2010, they'd be born in '93, making them a little too young to be in the same preschool class as Dean and Kris. Also, Nancy's birth year is shown to be 1992, making her only two years old when starting preschool with the others, leading to a whole bunch of confusion as to what year the film takes place and how old the kids are, especially since Quentin states that they were all five when they had a class together. If he's right about that, Nancy's birth year is wrong, as is Dean's age. Logically, the thing that makes the most sense is having them all have been five years old in '94 and '95, based upon Quentin's statement. It's a correct age for them to have been together in preschool, so it makes the most sense. Based on this, it would seem like the obituaries placing them at 17 years old would then line up, especially since they're all still meant to be in high school, making a 12-year gap between going to preschool and the current year. Noting that their preschool year ended in '95, that give us the most likely date of 2007 for this one, and that's just all far too confusing for one little film.

The ending of the film mimics the original in that the kids decide to bring Freddy out from the dream and into the real world, where he can be killed. Unlike the classic, however, Krueger seems to actually be powerless here, with no additional reality-manipulating abilities. After a short battle, he's killed with a papercutter. I want to say that it's silly but one of the other films had him die by showing him a mirror, so whatever.

Budgeted at $35 million, the highest of the entire series, the expectations were pretty high. But although its opening weekend was strong, earning back its production costs, it swiftly dropped in the subsequent weeks. At the end of its run, it had brought in $63 million in the US, and when international receipts were added in, the final haul was just under $120 million,[9] making this film the highest-grossing entry in the entire franchise. However, a strong critical drubbing, along with intense fan backlash, led to it having a poor reputation. Based on this, despite the financial success of the film, no plans for a sequel were made. Notably, it remains Bayer's sole directing credit in features.

Since then, the rights for the series have reverted back to the estate of Wes Craven, basically guaranteeing that any new follow-up would not follow the remake's continuity. Recently, it was reported that there's a possibility that Freddy would return in an HBO Max series, but that information is merely rumored, and no hard facts exist, so currently, the fate of the dream world is in limbo.

Timeline Summary

Original Timeline

A Nightmare on Elm Street—March 1981 (date extrapolated from year given in *The Dream Child*)

A Nightmare on Elm Street 2: Freddy's Revenge—Fall 1986 (said to be five years after the original)

A Nightmare on Elm Street 3: Dream Warriors—1987 (said to be six years after the original)

A Nightmare on Elm Street 4: The Dream Master—1988 (said to be one year before *The Dream Child*)

A Nightmare on Elm Street 5: The Dream Child—May/June 1989 (shown on graduation caps)

Freddy's Dead: The Final Nightmare—1999 (date shown on-screen)

Freddy vs. Jason—Fall 2003 (estimated based on date given on billboard)

META TIMELINE
Wes Craven's New Nightmare—November 1993 (shown on a script)

REMAKE TIMELINE
A Nightmare on Elm Street (2010)—2007 (date calculated from all those ages they gave us that don't make any sense)

CHAPTER 5

Leprechaun

Okay. Let's talk about the Leprechaun, I guess.

As it is oft considered the "black sheep" of the horror family, people tend to undervalue just how consistently entertaining the *Leprechaun* series is. It somehow manages to walk the fine line between not taking itself too seriously and still actually putting some effort behind the production.

The saga began back in 1993 with *Leprechaun*, which was both written and directed by Mark Jones, in his directorial debut. It featured Warwick Davis in the title role, then mostly known for playing Willow in the movie of the same name; since that film, his prospects had been diminishing, so he figured playing a horror villain would be a change of pace. At the time, he was the most prominent "name" in the cast, although costar Mark Holton had been featured pretty prominently in a number of comedies. But it was the then unknown Jennifer Aniston who would go on to the biggest fame, even if her nose would not.

The story involves Old Man O'Grady, who returns home from a trip to Ireland with a bag of gold that he claims he stole from a leprechaun, the same leprechaun that then shows up to kill his wife. O'Grady captures the Lep in a crate, using a four-leaf clover to seal him in, where he stays for ten years until his house is rented out by the Redding family, including the aforementioned Aniston. After accidentally releasing the little guy, he goes on a rampage, on the hunt for his gold, killing and terrorizing along the way.

The first film sets up some of the hallmarks of the series to come. It establishes the look of the Leprechaun, and his unending desire for his gold. In this one, he has a set of magical abilities that include minor teleportation, the ability to mimic voices, and reattaching severed limbs. His own severed limbs. He has no interest in reattaching the limbs of other people, and prefers to be the one to do the severing. His look is established with his classic, stereotypical leprechaun clothing and hat. He has an Abraham Lincoln look going on with short, shaggy hair, a wild beard that avoids his chin and cheeks, with no mustache, and his skin tone appears slightly greenish and splotchy. He also has the unusual character quirk of being obsessed with shoes, and shining them, a trait adopted from some folklores about leprechauns.

There are several moments that become important to establishing a sort of timeline here. The first is that we know there is a 10-year gap between the opening of the film and when the Lep is set free, and that he was locked away, trapped, for that whole time. There's no evidence of an actual date in the main movie, but it can be assumed from the style of dress that it's set in real time, and occurs in 1993. With that in mind, the introductory part would happen in 1983, with the green guy out of action from '83 to '93. Also, at one point in the film, when asked his age, he states that he's 600 years old, making him born at some point in the 1300s.

An interesting aspect of the behind-the-scenes of the film is that it was originally shot to be fairly family friendly. The violence was toned down and mostly off camera, and the intention was to shoot for a PG-13 rating. After seeing dailies, the producer's decided to ramp up the horror quotient and had them go back for reshoots, adding a few more gore-filled scenes and inserts to extend the existing attacks.

The finale of the film establishes the Leprechaun's weakness to four-leaf clovers. It is set up in the beginning as a method of trapping him, but it's later clarified that they act in the same way as a poison to him. After finding one in a patch of weeds, the clover is attached to a

The Leprechaun (Warwick Davis) makes his debut (*Leprechaun*, Trimark, 1993).

wad of gum and shot into the Lep's mouth, causing him to melt down and fall into a nearby well, seemingly ending his menace.

Leprechaun was released in theaters and did surprisingly well. Against a budget of $1 million, it managed to take in almost $9 million in ticket sales,[1] even though it barely cracked the top ten in its opening weekend and had mostly negative reviews. Although it could hardly be called a smash success, it was certainly profitable enough for them to go back to the well. Which would have been fitting and kind of literal, since that's where they left our villain. But it turns out that it wasn't, since, as you'll see, that well has nothing to do with the next film.

An early version of the script did, though, since it featured the return of Jennifer Aniston's Tory. In this draft, the Leprechaun would return to seek revenge on her, planning to trick her into marrying him. The producers attempted to get the actress back into the role by offering her $25,000, but by this time, she had started getting notoriety on *Friends* and decided to pass. Rather than discard this version completely, they decided to keep the concepts of the Lep seeking a new bride in the script for what would become 1994's *Leprechaun 2*.

Mark Jones, who wrote and directed the first film and created the character, didn't return for the sequel except in a producer role, and the job was instead passed on Rodman Flender, fresh off his gig directing *The Unborn*. None of the original cast returned, save for Warwick Davis, although Gabe Bartolos, the makeup effects artist who developed the look of the little monster, signed back on again.

This one starts off in Ireland, as the Leprechaun appears in a completely different ensemble and tries to marry the daughter of his slave, William O'Day, but is thwarted. Because of this, he promises to return in a thousand years and marry one of the slave's descendants. Curiously, this tiny introduction scene would be the only part of the entire main series to take place in the creature's homeland of Ireland.

So, already, a huge issue with the timeline occurs, since in the first movie, it's stated the Lep is 600 years old, but this flashback takes place 1,000 years in the past, and in it the creature says that it's his 1,000th birthday, so in the present day, the character would be around 2,000 years of age, much older than was previously stated. The story then introduces our setting and protagonists, as we're in Los Angeles and meet Cody and Bridget, the latter of whom is coincidentally part of O'Day's bloodline. The leprechaun emerges from an old tree trunk, dead set on finding Bridget and making her his bride.

While on Hollywood Boulevard, at one point a movie theater marquee is advertising the film *Sister Act 2*, which came out in 1993, which would presumably be the year that this film is then set, and if so, then the prologue would take place in 993 AD. Considering that this would be what we assume to be the same year as the first film, combined with the shift in location, it's likely that this is actually a different continuity, and a different leprechaun that just looks the same as the previous one. It would explain how it was able to make it out of that well, be restored from his earlier defeat, and relocate halfway across the country from the original's setting of North Dakota.

His appearance has subtly shifted, with his face losing its green spotting, his clothing appearing brighter, and his hair is both longer and now bald on top, creating the classic look referred to as the "skullet." Leprechaun's magical abilities have changed as well, as he has picked up a few new tricks, gaining the power to create rather complex illusions, as well as a form of shape-shifting. It's somewhat possible that the shape-shifting isn't actually an ability and is just him creating another illusion, and that both new powers are an extension of one new one, but it's never clearly stated—and, to be honest, probably wasn't considered during the making of the film.

Another drastic change is the overall rules of the Leprechaun and his gold, as well as his weaknesses. There's no mention of the four-leaf clover in this film, and although there is a passing reference made to his obsession with shoes again, it's glossed over very quickly. One big changed element is that if you are holding a piece of the Lep's gold, he is unable to harm you. At one point, Cody is holding a gold piece, and a

Part 2's Leprechaun (Warwick Davis) shows a refined makeup and costuming (*Leprechaun 2*, Trimark, 1994).

demonic go-kart that the villain is riding passes right through him. But the biggest addition to the character lore is his vulnerability to wrought iron, with even the act of touching it causing him extreme pain. At one point in the film, he is captured inside an iron safe, and resorts to trickery in order to escape. The conclusion of the film involves the evil sprite being stabbed with an iron rod, causing him to explode and seemingly killing him, or at least this version of him.

The second film was also released in theaters, but didn't quite make the same impression as the first. Expectations were a little higher, since the budget was doubled and the sequel would cost $2 million, but it managed to only pull in around $2.3 million overall,[2] which amounted to a pretty big disappointment.

That didn't stop them, and two years later, in 1995, Trimark moved forward with *Leprechaun 3*, although this entry would skip theaters and instead go straight to video, a more cost-effective move.

Before this film was even conceived, there was the thought to make a Part 3. Originally, they had intended to shoot the second and third films back to back and feature a continuing storyline. Titled *Trial of the Leprechaun*, it would pick up immediately after the events of the second film, with Cody being arrested for the Lep's murders. The film would detail the court case, while having the imp return to cause chaos in the proceedings. This version featured another character from the second, Ian, returning to make things difficult for Cody. This seems a bit difficult to pull off, considering he died in the second one by putting his face directly into an industrial fan, but this scene was added in reshoots. Originally, the character was meant to have a much softer death scene, in order to revive him for the third. After the notion of shooting the films back to back was scrapped, his scenes were altered and his death made more apparent.

With that plan changed, it was decided to take the third film in yet another direction. Again, the only remaining aspects of the series would be Davis in the title role with Bartolos on makeup, with Brian Trenchard-Smith taking over the director's chair. Smith had already had a pretty storied filmography from action to comedy, and had proved his horror chops with *Night of the Demons 2* and *Dead End Drive-In*. He brought a more comedic take to the franchise. Not that the previous entries were serious or anything, but the third film went in with a more over-the-top attitude.

Once again, there are no story links between this film and anything that had come before. At the film's onset, instead of being blown into a million pieces, the little guy is instead frozen in the form of a statue and taken to a pawn shop. There is a medallion around the statue's neck that, when removed, allows the Lep to return to life and wreak havoc. The setting has changed again, as well, with this entry being set in Las Vegas and centering around Scott, a new arrival to town, who has a streak of bad luck but eventually finds one of the leprechaun's golden coins. The coin, unlike previously, grants the holder a wish, and Scott wishes for money, which he quickly attains in a casino. Afterward, the coin passes from person to person, with the Lep in hot pursuit, seeking to complete his stash.

Like the first film, there's really no signs of any dates within the film to place it within a time frame, but considering the stylings of the surroundings, and barring any contradictions to the other films, it's most likely set in its release year of 1995.

As before, there are enough inconsistencies to suggest that this is not the same character we encountered previously, and is yet another leprechaun. Besides the fact that he's no longer exploded, nor trapped in a well, there are the inconsistencies with the properties of his gold pieces, and his newfound penchant for speaking entirely in rhyme. In the previous films, the character would occasionally have some lines in verse, but in this one, all of his dialogue is rhymed. He also gains some new skills, as he can sort of warp reality now. At one point, he is able to magically inflate a woman's body parts until she's a giant mass of flesh, and at another, he can create a killer sex robot. Besides that, there's a new wrinkle in that if he bites you, you will transform into a leprechaun yourself, as happens to Scott. After a bite, our hero starts to get splotchy

The Leprechaun (Warwick Davis) takes Las Vegas (*Leprechaun 3*, Trimark, 1995).

skin, patches of hair, and begins to speak in rhyme while developing an insatiable greed.

The biggest alteration to the series lore is, of course, his eventual Achilles heel. Again, no mention is made of four-leaf clovers, and iron is never brought up. Instead, we get the revelation that if you destroy a leprechaun's gold, then you destroy him as well. Unfortunately, if you do so, you also destroy all the wishing capability. The movie ends with Scott choosing to overcome his newfound lust for gold and burning the booty with a flamethrower, which then kills Lep and reverses the effects of the bite, restoring Scott to normal.

The budget was reduced a bit, but not quite back to the amount of the first film, with a price tag of $1.2 million. Considering the previous films had performed well on the secondary market, the hopes were that the third film would match that success, while skipping out on some of the costs involved in a theatrical distribution. The gamble paid off and *Leprechaun 3* became the highest-selling direct to video release of '95,[3] virtually guaranteeing further entries.

For what it's worth, *3* is actually Davis's favorite entry in the entire series. He enjoyed the humorous tone and setting, while admiring the directorial style of Smith, claiming that he was able to make the most of the smaller budget.

Because of the renewed success of the third film, adding *Leprechaun* to the roster of successful direct to video series, a fourth film was ordered, with Trenchard-Smith returning: the first person to helm more than one entry in the series. He continues to hold that distinction to this day, for whatever that may be worth. He would take the series, and the character, to a place that he had never been before: space.

There was this unusual trend that emerged in the '90s in which franchises would be obliged to have an entry that went to space. To be honest, it was really only four franchises, which doesn't really seem that many, but it's enough to be something that stuck out. Jason did it, the Critters did it, the Hellraiser squad went there, and now the Leprechaun would join the ranks.

Leprechaun 4: In Space released in 1997, two years after the third film, and would also go straight to the video market, skipping theaters. Along with the returning director, Davis continued in the title role, and Bartolos provided the special effects, which would drastically increase with this one.

The story this time revolved around a space princess of sorts, assumedly one of an alien race, being kidnapped by the Lep, but she actually makes a deal with him, before a team of space mercenaries blow him up. He's not dead of course, because ... and bear with me here ... one of the soldiers pees on his corpse, allowing the Lep to travel through the urine stream and into his body, where he hides until emerging from his crotch area later. That now marks the second time in this book that I describe a horror villain returning to life because someone decided to pee on their dead body, so I guess let that be a lesson to you. Once reconstituted, he starts to make his way through the ship's crew, including *Tool Time* girl Debbe Dunning and the great Miguel Nunez, Jr. Along the way, some additional chaos occurs with the use of a growth ray that expands the Lep to giant size, a cross-dressing cyborg singing show tunes, and a robotic scientist forced to become a part man, part machine, and part spider mutant that attacks the crew.

Once again, there's nothing that links this film to any of the others in the franchise, with the exception of Davis as the leprechaun character. There's no indication that this version is the same as any other that we've seen—in fact, this one seems to have always existed in space. We're told that the setting is 2096, about 100 years after the film's release, so it's definitely possible that one of the leprechauns from any of the other films managed to get off Earth in the time gap between the films, but given the tenuous links, it's more likely that this one, like the three before him, are separate entities.

Although his appearance remains unchanged, his abilities appear to be quite different. With the exception of being able to regenerate, as explained earlier, he doesn't even really show off any magical talents. He's even seen shooting laser guns in a very non-mystical fashion. In fact, the word "leprechaun" is never uttered in the film, and he's instead referred to as an alien and a monster. He's also less interested in gold, at least as a concept. Previous films showed him to be wholly concerned about his own personal gold and maintaining his existing treasure trove. This version of the Lep has grander motivations, and desires a much vaster wealth and power, looking to add to his treasures; scheming with the alien princess is the first instance of him working *with* someone. Previously, anyone and everyone was a victim or a target for him, so having him pair up with someone in his plans is a unique turn for the character.

This is also the first film in the series that doesn't really have a definitive end for the Leprechaun. After being blown up (in terms of size), he's then shot out of an airlock and blows up (in terms of exploding). However, the film had already shown him being blown to pieces, to no effect, and it continues to be the case here, as his severed hand flips the bird to our heroes, showing that his body parts are still sentient. I suppose the pieces of him floating through space are a sort of end to the character, but it's not as clear-cut of a death as the earlier entries.

From Part 4, the Lep (Warwick Davis) becomes giant-sized (with Jessica Collins and Brent Jasmer) (*Leprechaun 4: In Space*, Trimark, 1997).

Information about the budget is inconsistent, with some sources saying it cost $1.6 million with others saying $3 million, and since it was a direct to video release, there aren't reliable box office numbers to judge the film's success, but the reviews were generally fairly negative. Although, that being said, they were actually somewhat less negative than normal, with some critics appreciating the embrace of the over-the-top nature of the series and the comedic elements.

The secondary market results were enough for them to warrant continuing the series, since three years later, a fifth entry would arrive with 2000's *Leprechaun in the Hood*, continuing the pattern of taking the title character and placing him into a new environment. They took him to Vegas, and then to space, so the hood would be the most obvious next destination, especially with an increasing interest in "urban" horror films at the time. Brian Trenchard-Smith did not return to the director's chair, and instead that job went to Rob Spera, who didn't have a background in horror with the exception of the first *Witchcraft* movie, which launched a 16-entry film franchise that could probably be a book on its own.

With the absence of Smith, that left the only returning entities as Warwick and Bartolos. This episode returned to Earth, but instead of beginning in the present day, this one further hammers home the idea that each film revolves around a completely different leprechaun by starting off sometime in the 1970s. We know that it's at some point past 1975, since a character mentions *The Jeffersons*, and that series debuted in '75, and Ice-T manages to trap the Lep by using the magic medallion from the third film. The medallion represents one of the few times that any sort of continuity is used between the films, although it does not indicate that it's connected to that entry. In fact, the little guy is turned into a statue through the use of it, and then is placed in the office of T's character, Mack Daddy, where it remains until the time that the film is set. There aren't any dates present in the film itself, but it's pretty obvious from the clothing and vehicles that it's set around the time that it was filmed, so presumably 2000. That means that this version of the Leprechaun was out of action, frozen as a statue, for around 25 years, and would have been there through the events of the first three films, basically cementing that this is a new character.

He's set free in current times by an up-and-coming rap band trying to get their big break, only to end up causing chaos when they take something that belongs to the Lep. And that's where this one throws a new aspect into the formula, as he's after not his gold, but a magic flute. The flute has the ability to enchant anyone who hears its music, allowing the group to become successful, but both the leprechaun and Mack Daddy are hot on their heels.

Lep's appearance remains the same in the film, and his demeanor and attitude are consistent with the rest of the films, and there's even a scene where he speaks in rhyme. But that scene is unfortunately a moment in which the character has an entire musical number in which he raps "Lep in the Hood, come to do no good." Some people have referred to this interlude as one of the low points of the entire franchise. Others have referred to this interlude as one of the low points of music in general.

There are some unsavory bits added to the character in this one, which add an unnecessary sexual aspect. In one scene, he encounters a transgender woman who seduces him and the two are seemingly shown to be having sex before the Lep murders them in the middle of the act. Later, after recovering his flute, he is said to have taken up residence in a fancy hotel, with a series of women being sent up to room where they are reported to be raped to death. This side of the character wasn't really seen before, with the exception of attempting to marry in the second film, and apparently having at least an attraction to the princess from the fourth film.

Another minor bit of continuity carried over from the previous entries with the reintroduction of clovers as a weakness. At one point, the main characters chop up some clover and interlace it into a joint, with the intention of giving to the Lep to smoke. Oh, yeah, I forgot to mention that the leprechaun now smokes weed. That's a thing here. The

**Lep (Warwick Davis) in the hood, come to do no good (with Daya Vaidya)
(*Leprechaun in the Hood*, Trimark, 2000).**

joint, once smoked, takes away the imp's powers, although it does not
kill him as it did in the first film.

Oddly enough, this is the first film in the series in which they do
not kill the leprechaun in the finale. After a showdown in which almost
all of the main characters are killed, with the sole survivor being, uh....
Postmaster P, it appears as if the villain is about to be trapped once
again by the medallion, but the scene cuts to black before we see it happen. In an epilogue, we see that he has survived, and is still controlling
P, living on to rape more people to death, I guess. It's slightly disappointing that the one version of the leprechaun that they decide to show
winning at the end of the film is the rapey one.

At this point, Trimark Pictures ceased existing, as in 2000 it
merged with Lionsgate Entertainment, who took over distribution.
After three years, they decided to continue with the franchise. It's
important to note that up until this point, the series had sort of developed a formula for just taking the title villain and placing him in a new,
unusual environment. That tradition was originally going to be continued, as they brought back Rob Spera, who pitched two different concepts. One took the character to Venice Beach, and the other sent him
to a tropical island during spring break. However, the producers imple-
mented a mandate that the film would return to the hood environment
and once again feature a group of rappers in the cast. Spera didn't want
to make what he saw as being the same film again, so he bowed out,
causing them to bring Steven Ayromlooi to direct.

And so we got 2003's *Leprechaun: Back 2 Tha Hood*. It's notable that although this is technically *Leprechaun* 6, that number is never mentioned, and instead, on the box cover, the number "2" is accentuated. This gives the impression of *Lep in the Hood* being the first of a new series, and this one being the second part of that. But even with this being treated as a sort of sequel to the previous entry, the only returning components are Warwick and Bartalos.

This one goes a fair way to establishing itself as a soft reboot. The film starts off with an animated backstory, telling of a time in which there were a multitude of leprechauns, but they all went into a self-imposed exile, leaving the human realm. However, one stayed behind, driven by greed, and that's our boy. This implies lots of things, including the revelation that there are more than one of his kind that exist. Their leaving our plane of existence could possibly indicate that all of the movies are supposed to be a single continuity, although that makes little sense considering what we've already seen. The options it leaves available are that we're in a new and distinct continuity, in which our main villain is the only leprechaun around and this movie is our first encounter with him, or that the exile the other creatures have gone into was limited, and after a time they returned to Earth, and the other movies were some of them, but the leprechaun featured in this film has been around for way longer.

So many other elements strongly distinguish this guy as a unique entity from the others, and the most obvious is the overall look of the character. His bright green suit is gone, replaced by a darker, more gothic-styled jacket and waistcoat. Whereas previously, when having lost his hat, the Lep was shown to be bald on top, in this one, he sports a full head of hair. He also acts very differently, with more limited capabilities. He doesn't use magic in this one, taking a more hands-on and violent approach to killing as opposed to using mystical means. And, although the character remains in the hood, no mention is made of a magic flute, or his zombie fly girl army. But he does smoke some weed in this one, so there is that.

Instead, the film opens with the leprechaun back in search of his stolen gold, and he's banished through the use of liquid four-leaf clover. The film jumps ahead one year, and a new group of young people find his gold in an old building and try to use it to better themselves and their community. However, the Lep has other plans, as just getting a hold of his gold now frees him from his imprisonment. The finale of this one goes all out, at first setting Lep on fire, which of course doesn't actually work, but then they shoot him with hollow-point bullets that contain the liquid clover. This seems to work and drains the creature

Hitting up the bong, Leprechaun (Warwick Davis, left) and Victor Togunde) style (*Leprechaun: Back 2 tha Hood*, Liongate, 2003).

of his energy, almost killing him, but they run out of bullets. Thankfully, they're near a construction site, and they knock him into a batch of fresh cement, where he sinks and is incapacitated, although an animated stinger shows him digging himself out.

Once again, there's no mention on-screen of a date, although given the evidence in the movie with the style of dress and cars being driven, it's pretty safe to assume that it takes place in its year of release, 2003.

This would be our last taste of the Warwick Davis leprechaun, as he would then leave the role. Trimark decided to not carry forward with the series, due to decreasing profits; another entry no longer seemed like a good business decision, so the franchise was put to rest. During this time, Davis became a father and wanted to take on more heroic and less violent roles, and stated that he wouldn't return to the character if they decided to bring him back.

It took them 11 long years to do so, but then again, they kinda didn't. Remakes were all the rage in the horror world, and even though they were on the tail end of the trend, Lionsgate decided it was the right time for another go at the Irish imp. So, in 2014, the inevitable happened and we saw *Leprechaun: Origins*, which was actually produced by WWE Studios, the wrestling federation, and Lionsgate took on the distribution role. Oddly, even though the title would seem to imply a prequel of some sort, it was instead a reboot of the series, with no connection to the previous films. Directing duties went to Zach Lipovsky, who had just handled the sci-fi film *Tasmanian Devils*, and the role of the title character went to professional wrestler Dylan Postl, who was most known as the character of Hornswaggle. In his wrestling guise, Postl was in full leprechaun gear, and would wear a costume not too far removed from the one that Davis wore in the early films, so his casting seemed like an obvious choice.

Also, for the first time since the beginning of the second film, we return to Ireland, which seems a little unusual for a film series about a leprechaun, as we follow a group of four college students on vacation there. They end up in a little mining town, and are soon being stalked by an unseen creature. The backstory drastically changes here, with the town striking a sort of deal with the leprechaun in which they can take the gold as long as they continue to give sacrifices to it.

When the villain is revealed, however, it bears absolutely no resemblance to anything that has come before. For starters, the character doesn't speak, although it does seem to be somewhat intelligent through laying traps for its prey. However, it seems more animalistic, drastically less human in its behavior, wears no clothes, and has no magical powers. It's basically just a feral forest beast, stalking and killing its prey through the use of sharp claws and fangs, and drool. Lots and lots of drool. It's constantly filmed using a distorted filter so that you can't get a good look at it, making it very unclear as to why the casting of Postl was even necessary. With the way it's shot, the character needn't even have been a little person, and with no lines of dialogue, any stunt person would have sufficed.

Remake Leprechaun (Dylan Postl) or whatever you want to call this (*Leprechaun: Origins*, Lionsgate, 2014).

There's actually no visible date in this movie, as most of it takes place out in the middle of the woods, but considering the main characters' style of dress and language, it's pretty fair to assume that it takes place in the year that it was released, 2014. With no connections to any of the previous entries, the time frame doesn't greatly matter, as well.

As stated before, this version of the Leprechaun has magical powers, and appears to be vulnerable to anything that would kill a human being. The ending of the film has a pretty simplistic resolution as our Final Girl throws a gold piece in the air, distracting it, and then cuts its head off with one swipe of a knife. They do cap things off with a shot that reveals that there are multiple additional leprechauns in the fields, setting things up for continuing this take on the character.

That was not to be, though, since this version's reception was a bit of a disaster. The film was released in select theaters, and then arrived on the home market soon after. Detailed box office information isn't available, but *Origins* was immediately given overwhelmingly negative reactions. The current score for the film on Rotten Tomatoes, the review aggregate website, has the film sitting at 0 percent, from seven reviews. The audience score is only 11 percent, with most critics citing its stale story, generic characters, and uninspired creature design. Many fans were very upset with the lack of Warwick Davis, and didn't quite feel like Postl was given the chance to shine as the character, or even *be* the character.

The tepid reaction to *Origins* put the series back onto the shelf for quite a while, but the gap was much shorter than before, since four years later, in 2018, it was decided to once again call forth a little Irish luck with *Leprechaun Returns*. This time, Lionsgate teamed up with Syfy to handle production duties, with the intention of airing the movie on their channel, with a VOD release shortly beforehand. Steven Kostanski, from the film enclave Astron-6, was brought on to direct. Steven was fresh off the success of the horror flick *The Void*, and had built a reputation for making movies that would pay homage to their source material.

The decision was made to change the game quite a bit, and go back to the beginning. For the first time in the entire series, an entry would serve as an actual sequel and, like the *Halloween* 2018 film, would ignore all other entries in the series, only taking the first film into consideration. Of course, for the *Leprechaun* movies, this was nothing new. All of the movies ignored all the other movies, so that part wasn't unusual. The difference here is that, unlike the *Halloween* sequel, this one wouldn't actually discard any established continuity and could still exist with the same timeline as the others. Working under the premise that each film focuses on a different leprechaun, this movie is simply returning to tell an additional story of a previous featured one.

We're introduced to young Lila, a college student, who is on her way to fix up an old house. Our first indication that we're back in the world of the original film is the return of Ozzie, now significantly older, but of course not a lot wiser. He meets with Lila, and it's revealed that she's the daughter of Tory, the character played by Jennifer Aniston. The house that they're going to turns out to be the house from the original film, which Lila's family has purchased and donated to the school to repair. While visiting, Ozzie approaches the old well and is splashed by an explosion of slime from down below. This results in Lep bursting forth from within Ozzie's belly, causing him to exclaim that they killed him 25 years ago. Since there's no other time reference in the movie, and no mention of specific dates, if we stick with the original film taking place in real-time 1993, this one then occurs in 2018, and remains in real time.

The look of the Leprechaun is somewhat different, of course, because Davis again declined to return to the role and is replaced by Linden Porco. His outfit is very similar to the original, and his magical attributes have returned, as does his shoe obsession, a quirk that hadn't been seen since the second movie. The top of his head is back to being bald, and his penchant for speaking in rhyme is back, and he begins to kill off the sorority girls and their friends.

Besides Ozzie and a callback to Tory with a soundalike voice, there

The revamped look of the Leprechaun (Linden Porco) (*Leprechaun Returns,* Lionsgate, 2018).

are no cast connections to the first film, but they do keep the lore, since once again, they use his vulnerability to four-leaf clovers. They manage to blow him up by force-feeding him a bunch of it, but a new tidbit is introduced here, and it's explained that if any portion of a leprechaun exists, then he is not dead. Because of this, all of the exploded pieces become mini Leps and continue his attack. He's stopped again by electrocution and fire, but is shown intact and alive in the epilogue, making his way back to reclaim his gold.

Again, the concept doesn't negate any of the sequels, since it can be interpreted that each movie occurs in its own universe, and are unconnected to each other. Sort of a multiverse of leprechauns in which they get up to different shenanigans on different worlds. The other possibility is that they all take place in the same continuity, and leprechauns as a race are pretty much all the same. In this scenario, each movie takes place on the same world, but are different villains in different scenarios.

Returns was actually fairly well received for a Leprechaun film, and currently holds the highest score for the entire series on Rotten Tomatoes, even if that score is a mere 50 percent. Kostanski says that he would enjoy making a continuation of the film to continue the story, but no word has been given as to that happening. The director would have competition for bringing the franchise back, since *Saw*'s Darren Lynn Bousman has declared that he has an interest in making his own entry. Claiming to love the concept of taking the character and placing him in odd situations, he has stated he would like to see Lep get his hands on a time machine and head back to the Colorado gold rush. He has claimed that he wants to have Warwick Davis return to the role, and says that he will ensure that it happens, although no further news has developed.

Timeline Summary

Leprechaun—1993 (based upon year of release)
Leprechaun 2—1993 (based upon Sister Act 2 being in theaters)
Leprechaun 3—1995 (based on year of release)
Leprechaun 4: In Space—2096 (date shown on-screen)
Leprechaun in the Hood—2000 (based on year of release)
Leprechaun: Back 2 tha Hood—2003 (based on year of release)
Leprechaun: Origins—2014 (based on year of release)
Leprechaun Returns—2018 (stated to be 25 years after the original film)

CHAPTER 6

Scream

There are very few filmmakers who can say that they helped shape the focus of an entire genre. There are even fewer who can claim to have done it in more than one decade. Wes Craven is one of those filmmakers.

Back in the '80s, when slasher films were all the rage, Craven changed the course of the era with a little independent film called *A Nightmare on Elm Street*. It made him a household name as far as horror families went, but his greater success was still over 10 years away. After that franchise's central character had dropped in popularity, and the slasher craze had long since diminished, Craven would once again change the game with a blockbuster called *Scream*.

With a script by Kevin Williamson, it began life under the name *Scary Movie*, and the original treatment was just a more elaborate version of the film's introduction. After kicking it around for a little while, eventually a full script was fleshed out. It sparked a bidding war between several studios, with Miramax eventually winning out. Wes Craven was the early choice to direct, and he signed on immediately. It seems that he had already read the script before it sold and was interested in purchasing the rights himself, but by that point the price had gotten too high.

The film starts with Casey Becker making popcorn, in an intro that has now become somewhat iconic. Although it has since become a part of the public consciousness, it's hard to explain how unexpected that opening was. Drew Barrymore had been billed as the star of the film, and was the most prominently featured in all of the advertising. Having her killed off in the first ten minutes of the movie took audiences completely by surprise, reminding some of *Psycho*, which also murdered its lead actress early on.

After that point, the film focuses on a group of high school students—including Neve Campbell as Sidney, Rose McGowan as Tatum, Jamie Kennedy as Randy, Skeet Ulrich as Billy, and Matthew Lillard as Stu—and their attempts to survive. It's also played up as a murder mystery, constantly throwing red herrings at the audience, with plenty of quirky side characters like David Arquette's Dewey and Courteney Cox's Gale Weathers.

There's never actually a date given in the movie, although it's clearly in the '90s, most likely early to mid, based on the rarity of cell phones throughout. In fact, one of the characters having a cell phone is what makes them a suspect. There is another timeline point of interest in the revelation that one year prior, Sidney's mother had been murdered, and Sid had accused a man named Cotton Weary of the crime, as her mother and Cotton had been having an affair.

It sets up all the concepts that will be part of the series going forward. You get Ghostface, a very human killer in a long black outfit with a mask that evokes the classic Edvard Munch painting, *The Scream*. One of the film's biggest contributions to horror is having a villain that's very vulnerable. Ghostface gets punched, kicked, falls down, and just generally seems like a klutz at times. It also establishes the "don't trust anyone" aspect that future entries will also have, making sure to throw out as many of those red herrings as possible. But the biggest contribution is the addition of a meta commentary to the storyline. In the film, the characters have an awareness of horror movie tropes and how to avoid them, with varying results. It creates a world in which the writers can embrace the cliches of slasher films, while at the same time skewering them.

The other big element of *Scream* that's distinct, and will carry on to be a trope of the series, is that there are two killers. In the end, Ghostface is revealed to be both Sid's boyfriend, Billy, and his goofy friend, Stu. Although this reveal had been done before in slasher films, *Scream* was the one that really nailed it in terms of the mystery. In the finale, both of them are killed off in spectacular fashion, with Stu receiving multiple stab wounds and having a large TV set dropped onto his head. Although his death seems pretty apparent, many fans have developed theories to suggest that he did indeed survive this fate, and at one point there was the intention to bring the character back, as we'll discuss a bit later. Billy's death is pretty undeniable, though, since he's shot multiple times, with the final bullet landing directly in his forehead, while poking fun at the "killer pops up one last time" trope.

The original *Scream* was budgeted at $14 million, a relatively meager budget, and the film took a gamble with the release. It came out on December 20, right before Christmas, a time that's usually reserved for Oscar bait and family films. A horror tale at this time of year is very unusual, and it might surprise you to know that its opening weekend looked grim. It debuted at number 4 at the box office, taking in only

Stu (Matthew Lillard, left) and Billy (Skeet Ulrich) are revealed as the killers (*Scream*, Dimension, 1996).

$6 million, landing behind films like *Jerry Maguire*, with *Beavis and Butt-head* actually grabbing the top spot for the weekend. Everyone concerned with making the film was pretty disappointed, as it seemed as if it were doomed to failure; however, the following weekend, and for several weekends afterward, its take increased, and word of mouth and good reviews kept people going to see it long afterward, until it finally earned over $100 million.[1] This is a rarity for a film that never made the top of the charts, and in fact wasn't even second place. The highest spot it achieved was third place, but its consistency kept it going, turning it into a massive hit.

Of course, there was no way that a sequel wasn't coming after that, but no one could have predicted exactly how quickly and tumultuously it would arrive. In fact, preproduction on *Scream 2* happened while the first film was still in theaters and it started shooting in mid–1997 to be released at Christmastime the same year. This type of quick turnaround isn't unusual for a lower budgeted, less prestigious series, but for a studio film of this nature, it's pretty uncommon. Along with the rapid schedule, the original script was leaked online, causing Williamson to go back to the drawing board and drastically change entire characters and plot elements, coming up with an entirely new ending. Because of this, at times they were filming without a script.

Surprisingly, they were able to maintain a good amount of continuity, mainly due to the fact that Williamson wrote both entries. The survivors of the first film are now in college, with both Gale and Dewey returning to assist when a new killer emerges. The two biggest elements in this one in terms of the overarching story are the death of Randy, possibly the most shocking moment in the film, and the inclusion of Mrs. Loomis, the mother of Billy from the first film. It's established in that one that she had previously abandoned Billy and his father after finding out about Mr. Loomis's infidelities with Sidney's mother. After hearing about her son's death, she decides to get revenge by taking on the identity of Ghostface herself. She also recruits film student Mickey to help her out, filling out the series' quirk of having two killers.

This wasn't the case originally, though. The initial version of the script actually had three killers, with Mrs. Loomis being instead joined by Sidney's boyfriend, Derek, played by Jerry O'Connell, and her friend Hallie. This version featured a number of other changes, including the death of Dewey, and a finale in which Cotton saves the day, but then also snaps and kills Gale. Writing on this draft wasn't even completed before the script leaked to the public, forcing the eventual changes.

They continue with the meta commentary, only this time instead of pointing out the cliches of horror movies, they specifically discuss sequels and their tropes. It's a slightly smaller factor in this film, but still present, especially with the inclusion of a new layer of meta, the *Stab* films. In their fictional universe, a film was made, based on the events of the first film, complete with celebrity casting, and titled *Stab*. The opening of *Scream 2* occurs at a premiere for said film, and brings a few different avenues for them to parody themselves.

From a timeline perspective, this film does a lot for the series, since the very first shot is of a movie theater marquee showing the date. It states that the date is April 18, 1997, which is pretty precise, and considering the entire film takes place in a relatively short window of time, it gives us a setting of spring '97. Later in the film, Gale asks Sidney to

Mrs. Loomis (Laurie Metcalf) goes a bit nuts (*Scream 2*, Dimension, 1997).

comment on the past two years, which could mean two things. First of all, it could indicate that we're one year after the last film, just like in real time, and her comment about the past two years could encompass everything from the death of her mother through the first film ordeal up until now. Second, it could mean we're set two years after the last film and that Gale was asking Sidney to comment on the aftermath of the incident at the house. Considering that there was time for Gale to have a book published, and that they were able to make a feature film version of the events, I think the second scenario is the more likely, which would place the first film in 1995.

By film's end, Randy has been killed, Dewey has been stabbed once again but survives because what's a stab wound anyway, Gale is shot but survives because what's a gunshot wound anyway, and Sid once again defeats both killers, including placing a bullet firmly in the forehead of Mrs. Loomis. I guess it's an interesting point to mention that every single new character of note who is introduced in this entry is dead by the film's end.

Scream 2 was just as much of a hit as the first one, almost matching its box office exactly. It didn't quite match the original for longevity, but had a much bigger opening weekend, and made just over $100 million.[2] Even with a beefier budget of around $24 million, this still was a huge hit, clearing the way to continue the series.

By this point, the franchise was redefining horror films and had become the biggest horror phenomenon of the decade. A third movie was a given, and a script was developed to coincide with the second one. But a series of obstacles would end up delaying the film and upending the process. First of all, Kevin Williamson's new higher profile suddenly got him lots of new projects to work on, actually making him unavailable to provide a script. He did give a 20 to 30-page outline of what the story would be, but then Columbine happened, and the studio got cold feet about the direction the project was going in. There are a few conflicting accounts of what this original direction was. Some reports state that it involved Stu, revealed to still be alive and behind bars, using his notoriety to influence others to take on the Ghostface mantle and attack Sid. Other information states that the story instead detailed a new set of killings around Sidney, although at the end it was revealed to be a group of devoted *Stab* fanatics who staged the entire thing, and no one in the film would be actually murdered. But both of these versions focused on high schoolers killing each other, something Miramax didn't want to portray at that moment. The decision was made to take the action out of Woodsboro and move it Hollywood, and instead of featuring students, to focus on the killer attacking a group of actors. However, due to his commitments to other works, Williamson was unavailable to handle the new changes. Ehren Kruger was brought in to write the new script, completely revamping the direction of the series. And so, two years and a few months later, *Scream 3* was released.

The storyline here involves the making of *Stab 3*, meaning that a decent amount of time has passed since the last film. Considering that in that one, the *Stab* series was on the first entry, there would have to be time for the second one to be made and released, and for them to put this one into production.

As far as continuity goes, even though a new writer came on board, it remained fairly consistent. Gale and Dewey are once again having relationship issues, because that's apparently always a thing between them, and Gale has decided to have the worst hairstyle in history, with ridiculous bangs. Dewey has been hired as a consultant for the *Stab* sequels, and is in Hollywood. Sid has now moved further away, isolating herself and working as a counselor, helping abused women.

Ghostface is back once again, sporting the familiar gear and looking and acting the same, although one notable thing has changed. Now, not only does the character have a device that can make him sound like Roger Jackson, but that device can imitate anyone's voice. It's a strange addition to the character, since the earlier films had focused on the killer using technology in his killings, but mostly utilizing things that were available at the time. The voice changer box didn't exist then, and still doesn't exist in the form that they use it here, so it stands out quite a bit.

Because of that box and some other odd quirks, this is often considered to be the worst of the sequels. Those other quirks include a dream sequence, which really seems out of place in this series, and a death by

Gale Weathers (Courtney Cox) and whatever is going on with this hair (*Scream 3*, Dimension, 2000).

fax machine explosion. I know that the fax machine doesn't explode itself, but the combination of the fax and the gas leak and the ensuing explosion is just a little silly. And by "a little," I mean it's very, very silly.

The movie also features some bizarre, random cameos from Carrie Fisher and Jay and Silent Bob (Jason Mewes and Kevin Smith), the latter of which is particularly ill fitting, as they're not playing characters. They're literally supposed to be Jay and Silent Bob. It could be said that this was some sort of attempt to incorporate this film into Smith's View Askewniverse, since the comic duo does indeed travel to Hollywood in their film, *Jay and Silent Bob Strike Back*. It's been insinuated that this places those films and the *Scream* universe in a shared continuity. However, in *Strike Back*, the pair actually wander onto the set of a *Scream* sequel, helmed by Craven himself. Since the films in the fictional universe are called *Stab*, and there would not be a conflicting series with the same villain and alternate titles, it can instead by assumed that it's in a different continuity. That means that the Jay and Silent Bob here are alternate versions that exist in this particular universe, and again ... it's weird.

The other unexpected cameo in this one comes from Jamie Kennedy, even though his character was killed in the previous film. It's revealed that he, I guess, expected that there might be yet another killer that was planning a Part 3, so he made a videotape to prepare his friends for that eventuality. He apparently did not plan ahead enough to know that there would be a fourth or fifth (or whatever entry the series is on as you are reading this) set of killings, and make a corresponding warning for those.

Given the Hollywood setting, it should come to no surprise that the meta elements of the series remain intact, and in fact are intensified in this entry. This does lead to one particularly effective sequence in which they've built a studio set version of Sidney's house, which has the killer chasing her through it, evoking the first movie, but with the added element of the realization that it's just a set.

The biggest additions to the continuity, as well as the timeline, occur in the film's final reveal. It turns out that the killer is Roman, the director of *Stab 3*, which defies all logic in just so many ways. There's the huge revelation that not only is he the killer, but he's Sidney's half-brother! It seems that Sid's mother had a short stint in Hollywood and was raped by one of the producers she was working with. The rape resulted in a child, and that child was Roman. She gave him up for adoption, and he grew up finding work as a music video director, eventually discovering the identity of his biological mother. It's then revealed that he once sought her out, only to discover that she was married with another child, and also having an affair. This perceived rejection caused him to snap and Roman then convinced both Stu and Billy to become murderers and then just sat back and watched everything unfold. Then, after two waves of murderers failed to kill Sidney, he decided to finish the job himself. So, to be clear, he found out his mother was raped, but then eventually was able to have a fairly well-adjusted life, but clearly still had some outstanding issues, and yet he somehow made *her* to blame for it, and organized her death. Then, he somehow continued to find Sidney at fault for really nothing at all, and decided to plot her death, and that plot involved becoming the director of a movie based on the events that he organized, that also coincidentally was being produced by the man who raped his mother.

Yes. That's the story.

Beyond that, the more confounding part is Roman stating that he found his mother four years ago and set up the events that led to her death. Knowing that would have to have occurred in 1994, that would set this film in 1998. At an earlier point in the film, we see some production boards up on a wall that say June and August. Now, it's never clear how far into production they are, but based on these boards, it's clear that this is set in the summer, so we're in the summer of '98, a little over a year after the second film. While this short time frame is implausible, it's not exactly impossible. If you assume that plans for a *Stab 2* went into motion very quickly after the release of the first fictional film, you can assume that the second one came out just a year later, much like the release of the actual *Scream 1* and 2. Based on advance numbers, it's likely they greenlit the third part before the second film was even released, making for a very short preproduction window and allowing them to begin shooting very soon after the second one's release. It's a

Roman (Scott Foley) unmasks himself as the killer (with Lance Henriksen (*Scream 3*, Dimension, 2000).

little difficult to see it being possible, but it's also pretty implausible that one woman could be targeted by three different psycho killers over the course of a couple of years, so who are we to judge? There's also the possibility that the film is set in '99, during the summer, and Roman is rounding down, since it's possible it hasn't been the full five years yet.

The grand finale here sees all three of our main characters surviving, along with only one of the newly introduced cast, and Roman being dispatched, once again with a bullet to the head. And when I say that, I don't mean that Roman once again took a bullet to the head. I mean that the villain of the series took a bullet to the head. The first option would have been silly.

Roman being the killer makes this the only entry in the franchise in which there is a single killer, with no mysterious accomplice also unveiled. This wasn't always the case; in the early draft of the script, Roman had some help in the form of Angelina, one of the actresses in the *Stab* sequel. It was supposed to be revealed that she was one of Sidney's former classmates, jealous of the sort of fame she had acquired through her ordeals. Although this detail was changed before filming began, traces of the storyline can still be seen in the finished product, casting Angelina in a suspicious light.

Since this film was possibly considered to wrap up the trilogy, the ending ties the characters up pretty nicely, with Sid moving on from being a victim, and Gale and Dewey getting engaged. With the man who considered to have masterminded all the killings from behind the scenes dead, it appeared as if the threat was over.

Instead of the December releases of the two previous films, *Scream 3* received a February debut, often considered a softer window for new movies, and was graced with less than glowing reviews. This didn't hold the film back too much, since it landed the top spot in its opening weekend, earning $35 million, very good for a February, and went on to accumulate around $90 million in the US and $162 million worldwide.[3] Although this made the film a success, it was considered a disappointment compared to the previous entries, especially once the increased budget was taken into account. *Scream 3* cost around $40 million, close to three times as much as the first film, and almost double that of the second, so even making a strong run meant the overall profit would still be less. It seemed as if the fervor for the franchise was waning, and with its standing as a successful trilogy, it seemed like it was time to put it to rest.

And for over ten years, it did rest. But ghosts never die. And I guess Ghostface counts? Even if he's not really a ghost, I guess his face is. So in 2011, Craven once again returned to the director's chair for *Scream 4*.

Although Kevin Williamson did return for scripting duties, Ehren Kruger was once again brought in to do some rewrites during the shooting phase of things, including a drastically altered ending.

All of the surviving cast members would return to their roles, with Sidney, Gale, and Dewey once again involved. The only other returning member of the team would be Roger Jackson, as the voice of the killer, and I've never really pointed out just how odd it is that a voice changer has a consistent sound no matter who uses it. Generally, voice changers alter a person's voice in a certain manner, but if a second person were to use the same one, their voice would sound different. That's not so here, since whoever uses this brand of changer just sounds like Jackson.

This one establishes where the main characters have been for the past decade or so. Sid has published a very successful self-help book and is now doing a tour to promote it. Dewey and Gale have remained in Woodsboro, with Dewey becoming the town sheriff and Gale continuing her writing career. As expected, they're having some marital trouble, because that's apparently the only thing they know what to do with those characters. There are several new, younger cast members introduced, including some previously unmentioned relatives of Sidney, including her aunt and cousin.

When she arrives in town, Sid states that it's the anniversary, although never says what it's the anniversary of. Promotional materials for the film say that it takes place 15 years after the original massacre, which could possibly be talking about the death of Sid's mother, or the series of killings from the first film. Considering that the second option seems more likely, and that would be in 1995, that would make this set in 2010. The only other mention of a time frame in the film comes from Gale stating that she and Dewey have been married for 10 years now. If you assume that they got engaged in '98 or '99, but then got married in 2000, this would make sense for the timeline.

Of course, the meta factor still comes into play in this film, with the characters deciding that Ghostface is enacting the rules of a remake, pointing out the new, younger cast members and the recreations of the kills from the original. *Scream 4* also goes further into the movie-within-a-movie element, detailing the numerous *Stab* sequels that would come out in the gap between *3* and *4*, with the storylines no longer following the real-life events of Sidney, and instead focusing on new characters. Apparently, one of them involves some sort of time travel? I mean, you can call me crazy, but I would actually want to see that one.

The continuity of Ghostface is actually still solid, maintaining the classic look with no changes whatsoever. He may be one of the few horror villains to keep a consistent look throughout this many entries. Curiously, even though the killers in this movie are both revealed to be daintier and shorter in stature, he's still portrayed as about six feet tall and physically intimidating during the killing sequences.

In the end, it's once again revealed that the killer is a duo, and like the second film, is a dual-gender one. Sidney's cousin, Jill, played by Emma Roberts, was the mastermind behind the plot, involving her fellow student Charlie in her scheme. They bring a social media element to the story, with Jill obsessed with attaining online fame in being the sole survivor of another Woodsboro massacre. Her plan is to kill everyone else, including Charlie, and setting up another student as the killer, positioning herself as the new Sidney.

Originally, the film was supposed to end with a sort of cliffhanger. Jill would have effectively won, ensuring everyone else in the house was dead and being taken to the hospital. However, before being taken away, it would be revealed that there was one other survivor, but it would be unclear if that person was Sidney or Kirby (played by Hayden Panettiere). The eventually filmed finale, at the hospital, was a rewrite that was added by Kruger, a move that apparently upset Williamson.

The fate of Kirby was a much-contested point for a long while after the film's release. The character was extremely popular and audiences hoped she was still alive. Her body is never seen after her initial stabbing, so it was considered to be an unresolved issue. Some pointed to the fact that she was stabbed directly in the chest, a wound very difficult

Jill (Emma Roberts) tries to take over the franchise (*Scream 4*, Dimension, 2011).

to survive. Later, when Dewey is talking to Jill in the hospital, he makes a point to say that Sid is merely wounded, and also there. It can be reasoned that since he didn't mention Kirby, it was an indication that she was not brought to the hospital, and instead was sent to the morgue. The pot was stirred by Craven himself, who said that he had intended for Kirby to live, although without any on-screen evidence, it became a disputed point among fans.

Although it was hoped that the film would restart the franchise and kick off a new trilogy, it was a bust at the box office. In its opening weekend, it didn't reach the number 1 spot, losing out to the kid-friendly *Rio*. That film managed to collect $39 million, and *Scream 4* only brought in $18 million, less than half of that. Budgeted at $40 million, the same as the third entry, it ultimately only managed to gross $38 million in the US and closed out at around $97 million worldwide.[4] It was the series' first failure, and it remains the lowest-performing entry.

This disappointment led to the shelving of the future plans, and *Scream 5* was taken off of the agenda. The franchise would be dealt an even bigger blow just a few years later with Wes Craven's death in 2015. This would seemingly be the end of the road for Ghostface, although the fourth film did at least offer a final resolution, with very few outstanding loose threads to tie up. It appeared as if the saga would end there.

You already know it didn't. There was money to be made.

Over a decade later, in 2022, *Scream 5* would be unleashed, under the streamlined title *Scream*. Following the precedent set, arguably, all the way back in 2011 with *The Thing*, but then popularized by the 2018 version of *Halloween*, the decision was made to have the new entry be a part of the series, in continuity, yet keep the same title as the original film. Without Craven to direct, the team of Radio Silence, Tyler Gillett and Matt Bettinelli-Olpin, who had previously impressed with their film *Ready or Not*, stepped in take over. Although Kevin Williamson didn't write the new script, he did take on a sort of "show runner" role and gave input and guidance to James Vanderbilt and Guy Busick, the new writing team.

This time around, the movie focuses primarily on a new group of characters, mostly high schoolers, with connections to the previous cast. Our lead protagonist is Sam, who is revealed to be the daughter of Billy Loomis. It turns out that he slept with her mother back in high school, cheating on Sidney and getting Sam's mother pregnant. Billy died, presumably, without ever knowing about it. Sam also has a younger sister named Tara, who is still in high school, and her friend group includes twins Chad and Mindy Meeks-Martin, who are the niece and nephew of the deceased Randy. Their mother is Martha

Meeks, Randy's sister, introduced in the third film. Of course, mixed in with the batch of new characters, there are also the legacy characters of Sid, Gale, and Dewey, all returning. Since the last film, it's revealed that Sidney has married and had children, with her husband's name revealed as Mark. It can be assumed that this is Mark Kincaid from *Scream 3*, as played by Patrick Dempsey. Gale is now a news anchor in New York City, and she and Dewey have gotten a divorce, because once again, relationship problems are the only thing they know what to do with those characters. Because of the divorce, Dewey has moved back to Woodsboro, but has lost the role of sheriff due to his issues. The character of Judy Meeks, introduced in *Scream 4*, also returns, now taking on the role of sheriff, and is revealed to have a teenage son.

During the course of the film, the new Ghostface manages to get the better of Dewey, finally killing off the character. Both Gale and Sidney manage to survive, although both are wounded, adding to their collections of scar tissue. Judy is also killed off, along with her son, as are some of the new characters, although the twins make it through alive.

In a minor moment of continuity, a YouTube thumbnail boasts an interview with Kirby, stating that she did indeed survive her injuries in *Scream 4*. There's also another tiny nod to previous films in Dewey's house, showing a box of ashes of Tatum, his sister. This was a nice nod, considering that there was no mention of the fact of the murder of one of his close family members in the previous sequels.

Again, the look of the killer is unchanged, with the only addition being the introduction of a camera in the hood, in order to record the murders. There is a version of Ghostface shown in a fake movie trailer for *Stab 8*, in which the mask is a bright chrome color, but this is just part of the fictional universe.

Also intact is the meta commentary of the film, this time centered around the concept of "requels," lampooning the current slate of sequels that also serve as a soft reboot of the franchise. By introducing a new, younger cast of characters, while at the same time keeping the continuity and bringing back legacy characters, *Scream* works as a satire of this trend, while also participating in it. The focus on the fan commentary of the *Stab* series adds to this with the outcry of the direction of the fictional films, mirroring online criticism of horror.

The reveal once again gives us dual killers, in keeping with tradition, and it's shown to be Sam's boyfriend, Richie, and Tara's friend (possibly girlfriend), Amber. Their motivation is their anger with the direction of the fictional *Stab* films, hoping to make their own version, with real-life killings. The finale takes place in Stu's house, the same

Dewey (David Arquette) meets his end at the hands of the killer (presumably Mikey Madison) (*Scream***, Paramount, 2022).**

location as the original film's ending, with the sisters coming out on top and Gale and Sid going back to their respective lives.

Unfortunately, this is the film that throws the entire timeline into disarray. First of all, a character states that the last Ghostface murders happened in 2011, referencing the fourth film, which switches the timeframe for that one. Considering they never say the date, and there's never an in-film reference to the 15th anniversary, the only mention comes from the acknowledgment that Gale and Dewey had been married for 10 years, which can easily be accommodated by saying their wedding was in 2001. There is a pretty clear date given in this movie, however, since they state that *Stab 8* has recently been released, and a YouTube video discussing it is shown with an upload date of 2021, making that the year this entry is set. The problem here is that, at the very end of the film, a reporter states that it is 25 years, almost to the day, since the killings that took place there before, so she's referencing the end of the first film. If so, that would mean she's saying the original *Scream* took place in 1996. This sharply conflicts with the opening of the second film. If that theater marquee is correct in saying that *Scream 2* takes place in April 1997, then there's only about six months in between the two films, which seems unlikely considering that they managed to make the *Stab* movie and get it released in theaters. A six-month turnaround time just isn't possible. That leaves us with a choice of disregarding either the date given in the beginning of the second film or the date given in this one. The interest seems to be in having the first film take place in the year of release, so it would seem that they really want to run with that date of 1996 for that one, so in this instance, we're going to disregard the date from Part 2. This means that *Scream 2* actually occurs in 1998, allowing time for a movie to be made and for Gale's comment about two years to make sense. This then pushes *Scream 3* to 1999, but keeps *Scream 4* in 2011. This move allows them to maintain the notion of a 15-year anniversary in that one and makes this film set in October 2021, and keeps it as 25 years after Billy and Stu's attacks.

There is one other issue with the dating here. Considering that Sam is intended to be an unknown daughter of Billy Loomis, he would have had to impregnate her mother sometime before October. This places Sam's birth at some point in mid–1997, and the absolute latest that her birthday could be would be around July or so. Since this film also would take place around October, and it's 2021, this would make Sam 24 years old. The only problem here is that it's said that Sam left town when she 18 years old, and has been gone for five years, which would make her 23, an age that would be impossible, considering that Billy would have been already dead. It's possible that Tara was approximating, and that her mention of five years was actually six years, but five is just a more convenient number. I mean, Tara was in the hospital, likely on some painkillers, and not thinking straight about numbers.

The fifth film was a pretty big success, seemingly embraced by critics and audiences alike. It received a 77 percent fresh rating on Rotten Tomatoes, with most of the reviews appreciative of how much it were able to retain the feeling of the originals, even with a new creative team. It went on to have a strong $30 million opening weekend, higher than expected due to the surge in the Omicron variant of COVID at the time. It went on to achieve a worldwide gross of $130 million against a reduced budget of $24 million,[5] reversing the slump of the fourth film and restoring the franchise's reputation.

As of the writing of this book, a sixth entry has been announced and preproduction has begun. Few details are currently known, although a good portion of the cast can be assumed to be returning. One vital member who will not be returning is Neve Campbell as Sidney. Apparently the producers were unwilling to deliver her requested salary, causing her to pass on the role. Fans strongly back the actress, as Sidney is the primary character of the entire franchise, and deserves compensation to match that. Considering the position that her character is in at the end of the fifth film, it does seem like an appropriate place to part ways with the series. Her story has been wrapped up, she has been given a happy ending, and with the addition of the new characters, the mythology can move forward without her. It has also been stated that the sixth film will take place in New York City, so it's likely that Gale Weathers will play a bigger part of the tale. Courteney Cox has already signed on to appear, and it's been announced that Hayden Panettiere will return in the role of Kirby.

Timeline Summary

Scream (1996)—October 1996 (based on the "25 years" comment from
   Scream [2022])
Scream 2—April 1998 (based on Gale's "two years" comment)
Scream 3—Summer 1999 (based on Roman's "four years" comment)
Scream 4—October 2011 (based on dialogue from *Scream* [2022])
Scream (2022)—October 2021 (based on a YouTube video date shown)

Chapter Notes

Chapter 1

1. https://www.boxofficemojo.com/title/tt0080761/
2. https://www.boxofficemojo.com/title/tt0082418/
3. https://www.boxofficemojo.com/title/tt0083972/
4. https://www.boxofficemojo.com/title/tt0087298/
5. https://www.boxofficemojo.com/title/tt0089173/
6. https://www.boxofficemojo.com/title/tt0091080/
7. https://www.boxofficemojo.com/title/tt0095179/
8. https://www.boxofficemojo.com/title/tt0097388/
9. https://books.google.com/books?id=9CmmmwEACAAJ
10. https://www.boxofficemojo.com/title/tt0107254/
11. https://www.boxofficemojo.com/title/tt0211443/
12. https://www.boxofficemojo.com/title/tt0329101/
13. https://www.boxofficemojo.com/title/tt0758746/

Chapter 2

1. https://www.boxofficemojo.com/title/tt0077651/
2. https://www.boxofficemojo.com/title/tt0082495/
3. https://www.boxofficemojo.com/title/tt0085636/
4. https://www.boxofficemojo.com/title/tt0095271/
5. https://www.boxofficemojo.com/title/tt0097474/
6. https://www.boxofficemojo.com/title/tt0113253/
7. https://www.boxofficemojo.com/title/tt0120694/
8. https://www.boxofficemojo.com/title/tt0220506/
9. https://www.boxofficemojo.com/title/tt0373883/
10. https://www.boxofficemojo.com/title/tt1311067/
11. https://www.boxofficemojo.com/title/tt1502407/
12. https://www.boxofficemojo.com/title/tt10665338/

Chapter 3

1. https://www.boxofficemojo.com/title/tt0094862/
2. https://www.boxofficemojo.com/title/tt0099253/
3. https://www.boxofficemojo.com/title/tt0103956/
4. https://www.boxofficemojo.com/title/tt0144120/
5. https://www.boxofficemojo.com/title/tt0387575/
6. https://www.boxofficemojo.com/title/tt8663516/

Chapter 4

1. https://www.boxofficemojo.com/title/tt0087800/
2. https://www.boxofficemojo.com/title/tt0089686/
3. https://www.boxofficemojo.com/title/tt0093629/
4. https://www.boxofficemojo.com/title/tt0095742/

5. https://www.boxofficemojo.com/title/tt0097981/

6. https://www.boxofficemojo.com/title/tt0101917/

7. https://www.boxofficemojo.com/title/tt0111686/

8. https://www.boxofficemojo.com/title/tt0329101/

9. https://www.boxofficemojo.com/title/tt1179056/

Chapter 5

1. https://www.boxofficemojo.com/title/tt0107387/

2. https://www.boxofficemojo.com/title/tt0110329/

3. https://books.google.com/books?id=5AsEAAAAMBAJ&pg=PA76#v=onepage&q&f=false

Chapter 6

1. https://www.boxofficemojo.com/title/tt0117571/

2. https://www.boxofficemojo.com/title/tt0120082/

3. https://www.boxofficemojo.com/title/tt0134084/

4. https://www.boxofficemojo.com/title/tt1262416/

5. https://www.boxofficemojo.com/title/tt11245972/

Index